The World War II
Tank Guide

The World War II Tank Guide

Jim Winchester

CHARTWELL
BOOKS, INC.

Published by
CHARTWELL BOOKS, INC.
A Division of **BOOK SALES, INC.**
114 Northfield Avenue
Edison, New Jersey 08837

ISBN 0-7858-1229-6

Editorial and design by
Amber Books Ltd
Bradley's Close
74-77 White Lion Street
London N1 9PF

Project Editor: Naomi Waters
Design: Ruth Shane

Artworks courtesy of Orbis Publishing Ltd and Aerospace Publishing Ltd

Printed in Italy

Contents

Panzer II Ausf F Light Tank

In the 1920s and early 1930s, the Germans, forbidden to have any tanks under the Treaty of Versailles, built a number of armoured fighting vehicles (AFVs) with cover names such as 'large tractor' and 'new model vehicle'. These heavy vehicles had merit, but were too large for series production given the limited engineering capacity in Germany at the time. What was needed was a light tank that would be cheaper and easier to build and could serve as a training vehicle until industry recovered from the last war. A series of vehicles followed, mostly having a crew of two men and a single machine-gun in the turret. The Panzer II was a larger version of these early tanks with a 20mm (0.7in) cannon as the primary weapon. Armour plating was enough to defeat the anti-tank weapons and tank guns of the time, but the gun itself was not effective against anything but soft-skinned vehicles. The Panzer II was seen as a stopgap weapon to cover delays in development of the Panzer III, and was really only intended for training and reconnaissance use. As it happened, they were the most numerous tank in service during the Polish campaign in 1939 and over 1200 were available by the time of the Western campaign in May 1940. By this time, enough heavier tanks were in service to lead the assaults so the Panzer IIs were used in a 'reconnaissance-exploitation' role. In other words, they probed the enemy line and made attacks only where the defences were weak, calling up heavier firepower with their efficient radios. Despite their obsolescence in the face of improved Allied tanks, production of new versions, including flame-thrower tanks and conversions of others into gun carriages, continued into 1943 and 1944. One of the more famous vehicles based on the Panzer II was the Wespe (wasp) self-propelled howitzer.

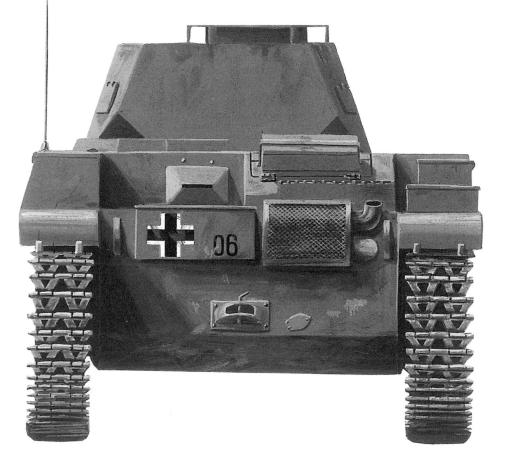

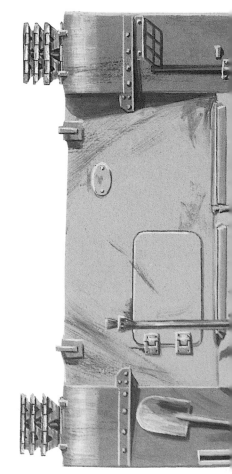

Specification

Country of Origin: Germany
Main Armament: One KwK 30 20mm (0.7in) cannon
Secondary Armament: One co-axial 7.92mm (0.3in) MG 34 machine-gun
Combat Weight: 9.5 tons
Length: 4.81m (15ft 9.5in)
Width: 2.28m (7ft 6in)
Height: 2.15m (7ft)
Road Speed: 40km/h (24.8mph)
Road Range: 200km (125mls)
Crew: Three

Panzer 38(t) Light Tank

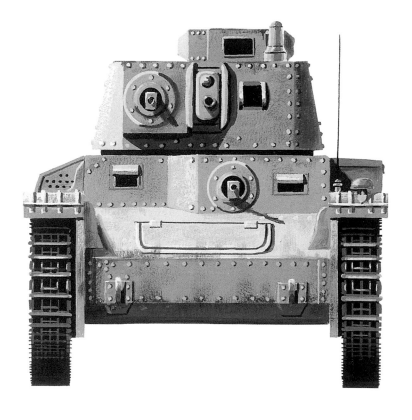

The Panzer 38(t) was one of the principal German tanks of the early war years although it was not a German design, being built in Czechoslovakia. The Czech army had ordered 150 of the LT Vz 38 light tank with a 37mm (1.5in) cannon in 1938, but the German annexation of Bohemia and Moravia took place a few months later before any deliveries could be made. The Germans took over the Praga tank factory and completed the order for themselves. One modification they made to the Panzer 38(t) (from Tschechoslowackisch or Czechoslovakian) was to make space for a loader's position, lowering the commander's workload at the expense of 18 rounds of ammunition. The first examples were designated the Ausf (Ausführung or model) A and many served in the Polish campaign. The next versions, (Ausf B, C and D) had minor changes of equipment but were basically identical. The first two of these served in France where their mobility enabled them to outflank the ponderous French tanks and penetrate their weaker side armour and tracks. After the Blitzkrieg campaigns of 1939–40, the Panzer 38(t) in its original form served on all fronts except North Africa. There were many adaptations of the basic chassis including anti-aircraft tanks, tracked howitzers and self-propelled guns. Some were exported to Hungary, Romania, the Slovak Free State and even Sweden during the war.

Specification

Country of Origin:	Germany
Main Armament:	One Skoda A7 37.2mm (1.5in) cannon
Secondary Armament:	Two Czech Type 37 (MG 37) 7.92mm (0.3in) machine-guns (one co-axial, one hull-mounted)
Combat Weight:	9.7 tons
Length:	4.54m (14ft 11in)
Width:	2.05m (6ft 9in)
Height:	2.36m (7ft 9in)
Road Speed:	42km/h (26mph)
Road Range:	150km (94mls)
Crew:	Four

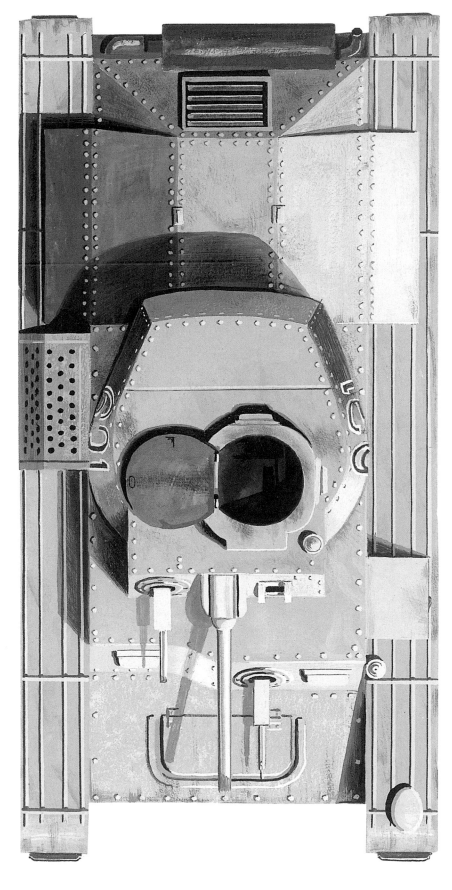

SdKfz 232 (8-rad) Heavy Armoured Car

Germany was an early exponent of armoured cars, partly because, unlike tanks, they were not restricted by the Versailles Treaty, and they were a cheap and quick way of mechanising the army and giving industry experience of building vehicles to military specifications. The multi-wheeled German armoured cars resulted from studies using trucks with drive on four rear wheels to achieve a good cross-country performance. Many of these trials took place at Kazan in the USSR under secret agreements. As early as 1929, three firms provided suitable 6x4 trucks that could be converted with new armoured bodies and a second steering position at the rear. Movement in either direction (as opposed to reversing) was specified for armoured cars in 1927, and this was adhered to for the next 15 years. Other requirements were for unaided trench crossing up to a 1.5m (5ft) width and ability to ford 1m (3ft) depths. Six-wheeled cars entered service in 1932 and served throughout the war, but had poor performance over uneven ground and so eight-wheelers were soon developed for the same purposes, but without recourse to commercial chassis. The most important of these, at least in the early war years, was the Panzerspähwagen (armoured reconnaissance vehicle) SdKfz 232 (8-rad). For some reason the ordnance department of the German army gave the same ordnance number (SdKfz meaning Sonderkraftfahrzeug or special purpose vehicle) to both six-wheel and eight-wheel armoured cars, so the vehicle here was suffixed '8-rad' to distinguish it from the 'other' 232, a similar car with a front-mounted engine and 6x6 configuration. For a vehicle expected to make first contact with the enemy, the 'Achtrads' were inadequately armed and armoured. The ability to change

direction (the requirement was to do so in under 10 seconds) can be understood in this light. They were excellent off-road vehicles however, partly because of their complicated but efficient all-wheel steering and differential system that prevented the inner wheels dragging in turns. In order to report their discoveries to panzer and other units, the 232 'Achtrads' were fitted with a large frame aerial for a powerful medium-range radio set, and this distinguished it from the otherwise identical SdKfz 231 (8-rad). Issued to the heavy platoons of the armoured car reconnaissance squadrons, the 231s and 232s were operated in conjunction with other vehicles, providing fire support when needed. The 607 produced saw service on all fronts where German forces were engaged during the war.

Specification

Country of origin:	Germany
Main Armament:	One 20mm (0.7in) KwK 30 cannon
Secondary Armament:	One co-axial MG 34 7.92mm (0.3in) machine-gun
Combat Weight:	8.3 tons
Length:	8.86m (29ft)
Width:	2.2m (7ft 3.5in)
Height:	2.35m (7ft 8.5in) without radio mast
Road Speed:	85km/h (53mph)
Road Range:	300km (186mls)
Crew:	Four

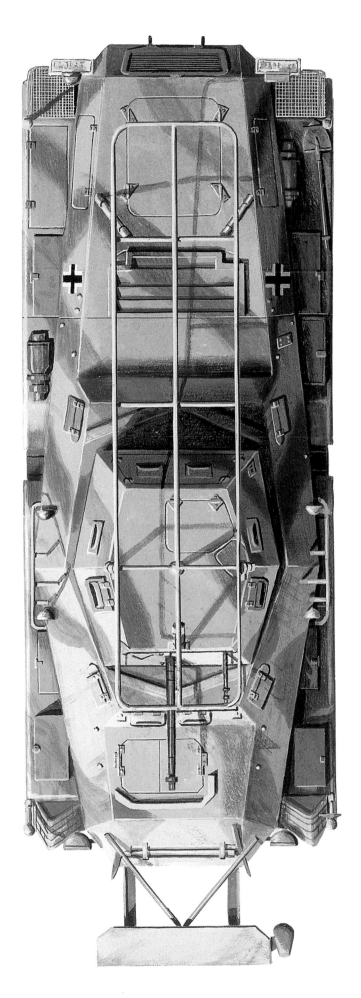

Panzer III Ausf F Medium Tank

German re-armament plans in the 1930s called for the new panzer battalions to be constituted of three light-medium tank companies and one heavy-medium company. The lighter tank, which was to form the bulk of the panzer force for much of the war and remain in production to its end, was the Panzerkampfwagen (PzKpfw or Panzer) III. One reason for this success was that a turret ring diameter was specified that would allow upgunning to higher-calibre weapons than the 37mm (1.4in) gun originally fitted. Development began as early as 1935, and the earliest models were available by 1937, seeing service in the Polish campaign. Despite problems with the suspension and thin armour, the Panzer III defeated all opposition in the Blitzkrieg campaigns, its only significant losses caused by Polish anti-tank guns. The first four models (Ausf A, B, C and D) differed mainly in suspension details. The Ausf E introduced the definitive six-wheel main suspension and had thicker armour, and the Ausf F (illustrated here) was basically similar. The first truly mass-produced version was the Ausf G, introduced in spring 1940: 600 of these were built, compared with a total of 601 of all previous versions. The Ausf H was the first model to introduce a heavier main armament – a 50mm (1.9in) KwK L/42 cannon – on the production line, although this was also fitted to later Ausf Gs, production of which continued in parallel. Many Ausf Fs, including this one, were retrofitted with features of the Ausf H, such as the turret basket and the 50mm (1.9in) cannon. Additional armour was built into the H and added to many Fs and Gs. The only reliable way to identify an upgraded F or G was by reference to the sprocket wheel, which had eight holes rather than the six on the H and later models. Panzer IIIs with the 50mm gun were the most effective tank in the early part of the North African campaign, able to defeat all Allied tanks until the arrival of the Sherman. In the invasion of the USSR in 1941, this gun was rendered obsolete by the Soviet T-34. Subsequent models were fitted with a long-barrelled 75mm (2.9in) cannon that had a chance of outranging Soviet tanks. Production of the basic Panzer III models continued into July 1943, but assault guns and other derivatives were produced until May 1945.

Specification

Country of origin:	Germany
Main Armament:	One 50mm (1.9in) KwK L/42 cannon
Secondary Armament:	Two 7.92mm (0.3in) MG 34 machine-guns (one on hull, one co-axial)
Combat Weight:	21.8 tons
Length:	5.41m (17ft 9in)
Width:	2.95m (9ft 6in)
Height:	2.44m (8ft)
Road Speed:	40km/h (25mph)
Road Range:	163km (186mls)
Crew:	Five

Panzer IV Ausf F1 Medium Tank

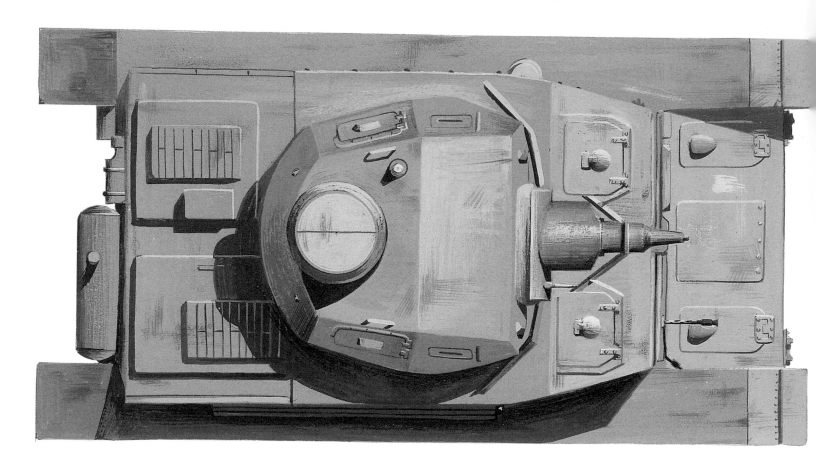

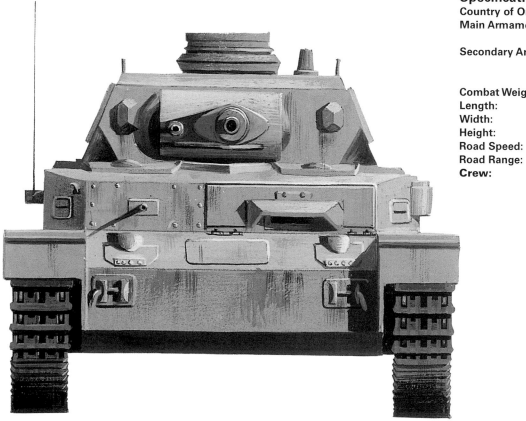

Specification

Country of Origin: Germany
Main Armament: One 75mm (2.9in) KwK 37 cannon
Secondary Armament: Two 7.92mm (0.3in) MG 34 machine-guns (one on hull, one on turret roof)
Combat Weight: 22.3 tons
Length: 5.92m (19ft 5in)
Width: 2.84m (9ft 4in)
Height: 2.68m (8ft 7in)
Road Speed: 42km/h (26mph)
Road Range: 200km (124mls)
Crew: Five

The Panzer IV was developed in the mid-1930s to fulfil German army plans for the fourth 'heavy' company in the panzer divisions then being secretly formed by the Nazis. In 1938, when the first examples were delivered, the only western tanks with firepower to match it were obsolescent French models with tactically inefficient hull-mounted guns. Only 211 had been completed by the outbreak of war in September 1939. By May 1940, there were 280 of the first four models (Ausf A–D) available to the forces poised to invade France and the Low Countries. The Panzer IV (which predated the Panzer III into production) set the pattern for battle tanks up to the present day, with a centrally mounted rotating turret mounting a heavy gun armament and a co-axial machine-gun, a commander's cupola allowing 360 degree vision, a rear-mounted engine and a forward compartment for the driver and radio operator. Most of these features had appeared on various earlier tanks, but the impact of the German medium panzers between 1939 and 1940 meant that almost all subsequent medium and heavy tanks have followed the same basic principles. Early models were armed with the short-barrelled KwK 37 L/24 75mm (3in) gun, but this was outranged by the 76mm (2.9in) guns of the Soviet T-34s and later models of the Panzer IV Ausf F (usually known as Ausf F2) were fitted with the long-barrelled KwK 40 L/43 with a muzzle velocity of 700m/s (766yds/s). The version illustrated is an Ausf F1 with increased (up to 50mm/1.9in) armour over previous versions, a modified turret, wider tracks and intakes on the glacis plate for brake cooling. A total of 462 were produced (from a total of over 9000 Panzer IVs of all variants) and they served in North Africa, the Balkans and the Soviet Union. Between June 1942 and July 1943, Ausf F1 strength on the Eastern front dropped from 208 to 60, and before long it had faded from the scene.

Panzer VI Ausf H Tiger Heavy Tank

The Tiger was the most famous of all German tanks. Specifications for what was to become the Tiger were issued as early as 1937, but this 'breakthrough tank' project was cancelled after some test models were built by Henschel. In 1941 the design was dusted off when a new requirement for a heavy tank mounting an 88mm (3.5in) gun was issued. This requirement was changed at least twice before prototypes were ordered from both Henschel and Porsche which were to be demonstrated before Hitler on his birthday on 20 April 1942. Both designs were quite similar and both were given production orders, as the Panzer VI Tiger and the Tiger (P) (for Porsche). The Henschel model was superior, easier to produce and was not beset with the technical problems that dogged the Porsche tank. It was chosen for large-scale production and rushed into service in August 1942 to participate in the attack on Leningrad where it was used in unsuitable terrain and soon picked out for special attention by the anti-tank gunners. Little more success was achieved in Tunisia soon afterwards, although the design of the Tiger aroused great interest among Allied armies. The Tiger's heyday was in Normandy after the Allied landings when the very suggestion that there were Tigers (or a Tiger) about was enough to cause 'Tiger Terror' and hold up an advance. The Tiger simply had better armour and a better gun than any British or American tank it faced in 1944. A well-handled Tiger was known to destroy a dozen opposing tanks in a single engagement, and if lucky, might be able to withdraw to fight again. Despite its capabilities, it was complex, unwieldy and vulnerable to attack from the rear. The innovative interleaving road wheels were prone to clogging with mud, which often froze overnight and immobilised the Tiger. Production ended in August 1944 after 1354 were produced, but Tigers fought on until the last were encircled in Berlin in May 1945.

Specification

Country of Origin:	Germany
Main Armament:	One 88mm (3.5in) KwK 36 cannon
Secondary Armament:	Two 7.92mm (0.3in) MG 34 machine-guns (one co-axial, one hull-mounted)
Combat Weight:	56 tons
Length:	8.26m (27ft 9in)
Width:	2.82m (9ft 3in)
Height:	2.86m (9ft 5in)
Road Speed:	37km/h (23mph)
Road Range:	117km (73mls)
Crew:	Five

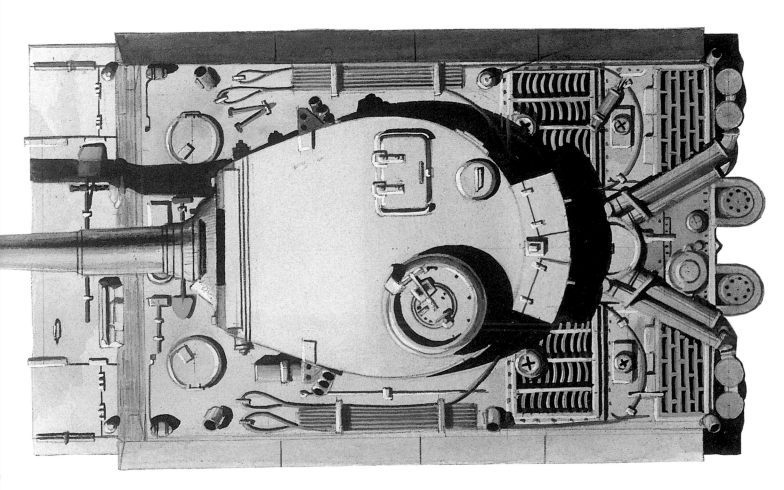

Panzer III Ausf J (special) Medium Tank

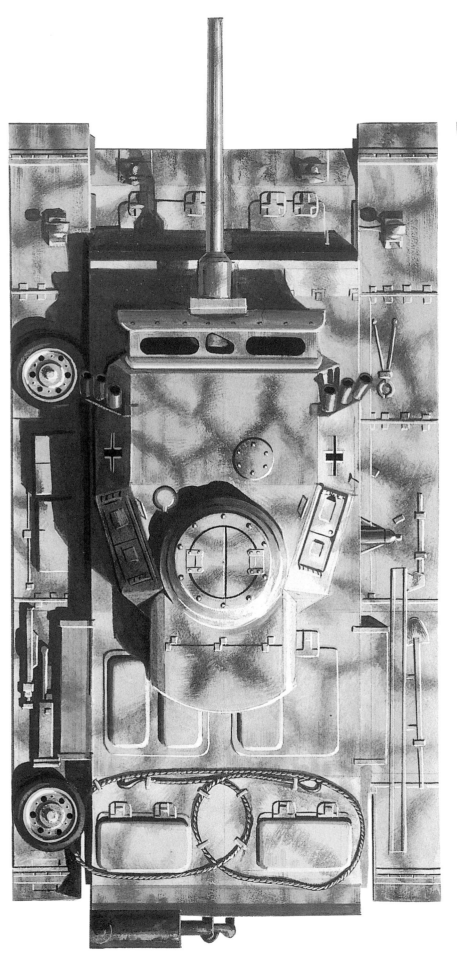

Specification

Country of Origin:	Germany
Main Armament:	One 50mm (1.9in) KwK 30 L/60 cannon
Secondary Armament:	Two MG 34 7.92mm (0.3in) machine-guns (one co-axial, one hull-mounted)
Combat Weight:	21.5 tons
Length:	6.28m (20ft 7in)
Width:	2.95m (9ft 8in)
Height:	2.5m (8ft 2in)
Road Speed:	40km/h (25mph)
Road Range:	155km (96mls)
Crew:	Five

In 1942 Allied forces in North Africa encountered a hitherto unknown type of Panzer III with a new type of long-barrelled gun. This gun had the same 50mm (1.9in) calibre as the guns fitted on the current model (Ausf J) Panzer IIIs but was significantly longer, harder hitting and more accurate. The new gun proved able to knock out even the larger British and US-built tanks then in service at a range where the Allies' tank guns were ineffective. Otherwise the tanks were identical to other Ausf Js. The Allies dubbed these new tanks 'specials'. This development was not radical, but was timely in that it arrived on the North African and Russian battlefields at a moment when current guns were proving inadequate. Its introduction was postponed by a rare example of anyone ignoring an order by Hitler. In August 1940, the Führer, who interfered in many things but took a particular interest in tank armament, had seen the new long-barrelled (60 calibres) 50mm (1.9in) KwK 30 cannon and ordered that it be fitted to the Panzer III. The ordnance department did not implement this order, being satisfied with the performance of the recently introduced 45-calibre gun, but when the Panzer III with the big gun did not show up at his traditional birthday parade in April 1941, Hitler noticed and insisted its fitting be instituted as soon as possible. In early 1942, Ausf Js with the new gun were issued to motorised infantry detachments as their main equipment. Many others went to fill gaps in the Eastern Front panzer battalions that had been hard hit in late 1941 when the Soviets had regrouped. Although the higher muzzle velocity – and thus penetrating power – of the longer gun was welcome, the 'specials' had no more chance of defeating a T-34 in a frontal attack than did their predecessors. Production of the Ausf J with the long gun amounted to 1067. This compares to 1549 with the 'standard' gun.

Leichter Flakpanzer 38(t) Light Anti-aircraft Tank

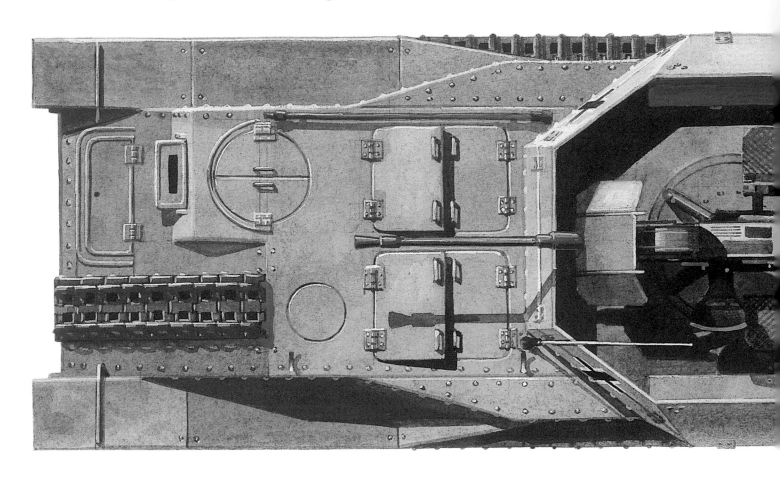

Based on the versatile Czech-built Panzer 38(t) chassis, the Leichter Flakpanzer (light anti-aircraft tank) was the first fully tracked self-propelled anti-aircraft vehicle. It was developed as a makeshift solution to the urgent need for anti-aircraft support for the Panzer regiments after Hitler refused to allow Panzer IVs to be fitted with a quadruple 20mm (1.5in) mount. The 37mm (0.7in) gun turret of the standard Panzer 38(t) was replaced by a rear-mounted octagonal shield made of 10mm (0.3in) armour plate. The upper portions of the gun shield hinged outwards and were opened up when the gun was in action for better access to the gun and for traverse against targets at low angles. The gun was traversed by hand and was supplied with up to 360 rounds of ammunition stored within the vehicle. One hundred and fifty SdKfz 140 Leichte Flakpanzer were ordered in late 1943, but only 140 were converted due to disappointment with the vehicle's lack of firepower and the development of newer vehicles with dual and quadruple mounts. Issued to the flak platoons of panzer regiments in early 1944, this vehicle saw most use on the Western Front, notably in Normandy with the 12th SS Division.

Specification

Country of Origin:	Germany
Main Armament:	One 20mm (0.7in) Flak 38 anti-aircraft gun
Secondary Armament:	None
Combat Weight:	9.8 tons
Length:	4.61m (15ft 1in)
Width:	2.15m (7ft 1in)
Height:	2.25m (7ft 5in)
Road Speed:	42km/h (26mph)
Road Range:	210km (130mls)
Crew:	Four

SdKfz 135/1 Lorraine Schlepper Self-propelled Heavy Howitzer

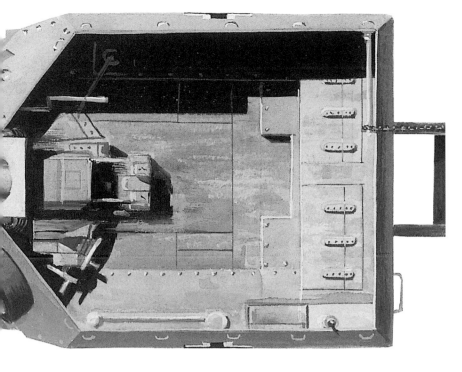

Specification

Country of Origin:	Germany
Main Armament:	sFH13 150mm (5.9in) howitzer
Secondary Armament:	None
Combat Weight:	8.49 tons
Length:	5.31m (17ft 5in)
Width:	1.83m (6ft)
Height:	2.23m (7ft 4in)
Road Speed:	34km/h (21.1mph)
Road Range:	135km (84mls)
Crew:	Four

One of a number of German 'lash-ups' developed in the race to produce a useful mobile anti-tank gun, the Lorraine Schlepper was based on captured French chassis combined with an old World War I artillery piece. The German haul of French equipment after the fall of France in 1940 included over 300 Tracteur Blindé 37Ls which were a tracked general purpose carrier similar to, but larger than, the British Universal (Bren) carrier. Withdrawn from stockpile in early 1942 for the Panzerjäger (tank hunter) project, 40 of these vehicles were instead converted on Hitler's orders to carry a 150mm (5.9in) howitzer for special operations with Rommel's Afrika Korps and these were issued to the 21st Panzer Division. The majority of conversions were made in Paris using superstructures supplied by the German Alkett company although at least 30 were converted at Krefeld. As an alternative, the 105mm (4.1in) leFH18/40 howitzer could be fitted although it appears that only 12 of a proposed 60 were fitted with this gun. At least one was fitted with a Russian 122mm (4.8in) howitzer and incorporated into an armoured train which was captured in France in late 1944. It is believed that 94 Lorraine Schleppers were eventually produced with the 150mm (5.9in) gun. The gun itself could be elevated up to 40 degrees and the armoured superstructure could contain eight rounds of ammunition as well as the crew of four. At the rear was a large recoil spade that dug into the earth when the gun fired. Vehicles overhauled in 1944 incorporated the larger spade seen here which could be raised and lowered without the crew having to leave the fighting compartment.

Sturmgeschütz III Ausf G Assault Gun

The Sturmgeschütz (StuG) III Ausf G was the last in a long series of basically similar 75mm (2.9in) assault guns based on the Panzer III. These began with the StuG Ausf A of 1940 and proceeded through four major variants before the definitive StuG III Ausf (model) G began to leave the factory in December 1942. Models up to the Ausf F had a short-barrelled (24-calibres) gun, but the F and G toted a 48-calibres gun with muzzle brake in an attempt to regain superiority over the Soviet types being encountered for the first time, namely the KV-1 and T-34. This gun was a development of the PaK 40 towed anti-tank gun and signalled a change in role for the StuGs which had been designed for assault of buildings and fortifications in conjunction with infantry. Tank production had not kept up with losses and demands of the expanding Eastern Front and the assault guns were called in to operate alongside the panzers in conventional tank versus tank engagements. Features of the Ausf G included a cupola with periscopes to give the commander some protection while he surveyed the terrain, slanted plates protecting the front of the side panniers, and a machine-gun with shield mounted in front of the loader's hatch. The early StuGs had no secondary armament and the Ausf F had a machine-gun stowed inside that had to be brought out and fired from an exposed position. In 1944, a co-axial machine-gun was finally added, as was a remote-controlled gun for the turret roof. Side skirts and Zimmerit coating were factory-applied to later production examples. The low profile and mechanical reliability of the StuGs saw their employment throughout the war and their adaptation to other uses such as flame-throwers and ammunition-carriers. Their utility is seen in the production figures: 8587 StuG IIIs were produced, together with over 800 earlier versions.

Specification

Country of Origin:	Germany
Main Armament:	One 75mm (2.9in) StuK 40 cannon
Secondary Armament:	One 7.92mm (0.3in) MG 42 machine-gun on roof
Combat Weight:	23.9 tons
Length:	6.77m (22ft 2in)
Width:	2.95m (9ft 8in)
Height:	2.16m (7ft 2in)
Road Speed:	40km/h (25mph)
Road Range:	155km (96mls)
Crew:	Four

SdKfz 234/2 Puma Armoured Car

The Germans made much use of wheeled armoured cars in their reconnaissance battalions for scouting out enemy positions. The best of these was the eight-wheeled SdKfz 234 series which combined high speed, long range and, in later variants, big hitting power for their size. The SdKfz 234/2 Puma as it became known, was the descendent of earlier 'Achtrads' (8-wheeler) vehicles equipped mainly with 20mm (0.7in) cannon armament, but was of monocoque construction with the hull forming the chassis. A fully enclosed turret designed originally for the abandoned Leopard light tank was fitted and this carried a long-barrelled 50mm (1.9in) cannon which could defeat most enemy reconnaissance vehicles, the Puma's most common adversary. The gun mantlet provided extra ballistic protection and was of the 'Saukopf' (sow's head) variety fitted to many late-war German vehicles. The development of the Puma was protracted as it was intended for use in North Africa, but that war was over by the time problems with 'tropicalising' the vehicle had been solved. The first vehicles saw combat on the Eastern Front where their great range proved invaluable, although they were complex to maintain and hard to support a long way from maintenance depots. The Pumas were all-wheel drive and all-wheel steering (necessary to prevent the rear wheels dragging in the turn). There was a second backward-facing driving position ahead of the engine which, together with a gearbox with six forward and six reverse gears, enabled the Puma to be driven equally fast in either direction, an advantage for a reconnaissance vehicle that was designed to observe and report as fast as possible. The heavy main armament, however, tended to encourage Puma crews to engage the enemy, thus defeating the original purpose. Only 101 of the turreted 234/2 Pumas were built. They were followed by similar numbers of 234/3s and 234/4s, which mounted various anti-tank guns in open-topped superstructures.

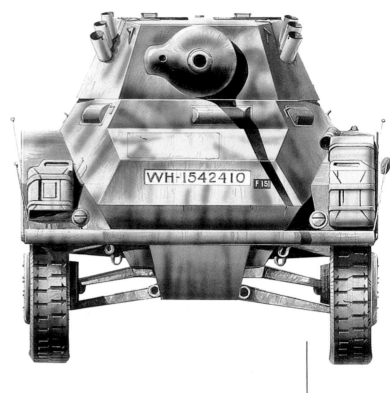

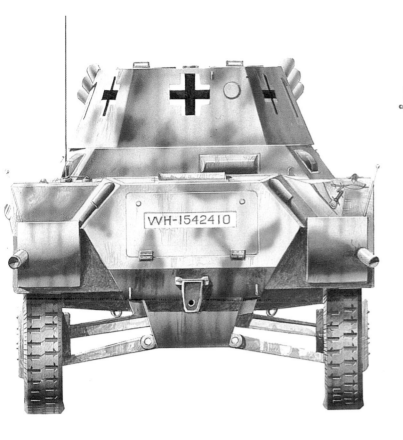

Specification

Country of Origin:	Germany
Main Armament:	One 50mm (1.9in) KwK 39/1 cannon
Secondary Armament:	One co-axial 7.92mm (0.3in) MG 42 machine-gun
Combat Weight:	11.74 tons
Length:	6.80m (22ft 4in); hull length: 6m (19ft 8in)
Width:	2.33m (7ft 7in)
Height:	2.38m (7ft 10in)
Road Speed:	85km/h (53mph)
Road Range:	550km (350mls)
Crew:	Four

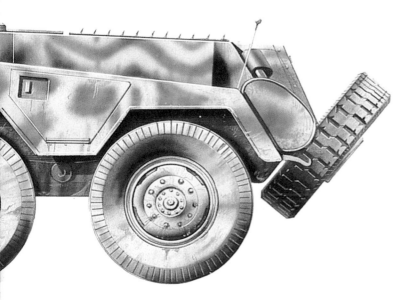

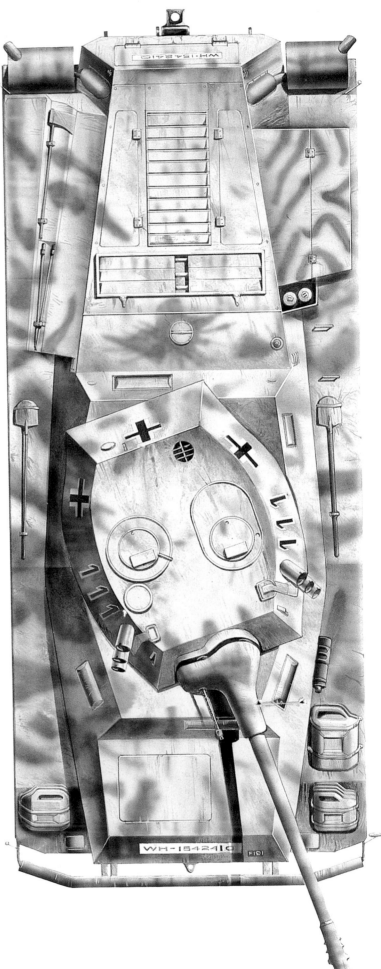

Sturmpanzer IV Brummbär Assault Gun

The Sturmpanzer IV was a variation on the standard Panzer IV for providing mobile artillery support to infantry. The new superstructure was designed by the Alkett firm to mount a 150mm (5.9in) howitzer and when Hitler saw the plans in October 1942 he ordered that 40 to 60 be built immediately. When this batch was completed in May 1943, series production was ordered and continued to the end of the war, by which time a total of 298 had been completed. The high box-like superstructure housed a Sturmhaubitze (assault howitzer) L/12 in a ball mount with frontal armour of 100mm (3.9in) and side armour of 50mm (0.2in). After 1943 additional armour in the form of Schürzen (skirts) was usually fitted as seen here. This was simply 5mm (0.2in) mild-steel boilerplate attached by brackets to protect the hull against hollow-charge weapons which would thus expend their energy well clear of the interior. Assault tank battalion 216 was the first unit equipped with the SdKfz 166 Brummbär (grizzly bear) and went into action at Kursk in July 1943. A lack of self-protection guns proved a disadvantage, but the mechanical reliability and general soundness of the Panzer IV chassis allowed them to avoid the fate of many newer designs in that battle which were unable to outmanoeuvre the enemy or just broke down. On the other hand, the Brummbär was rather heavy and slow, not a real problem in its intended role of providing heavy fire against fixed positions at the forefront of an infantry assault,

but a liability in any sort of defensive fighting or against enemy armour. Later production Brummbärs had a periscope for the driver as seen here rather than a direct-vision visor. The final models remedied the deficiencies in self-defence by adding a ball-mounted machine-gun in the upper-left of the front face. A commander's cupola with an MG 34 for anti-aircraft defence was another late addition. After its debut on the Russian front, three more assault tank battalions were equipped with the Brummbär and fought on the Western Front and in Italy.

Specification

Country of Origin:	Germany
Main Armament:	One 150mm (5.9in) StuH 43 howitzer
Secondary Armament:	None on early models
Combat Weight:	28.2 tons
Length:	5.93m (19ft 5in)
Width:	2.88m (9ft 5in)
Height:	2.52m (8ft 3in)
Road Speed:	40km/h (25mph)
Road Range:	210km (130mls)
Crew:	Five

Leichte Feldhaubitze 18/2 auf Fahrgestell Panzerkampfwagen II

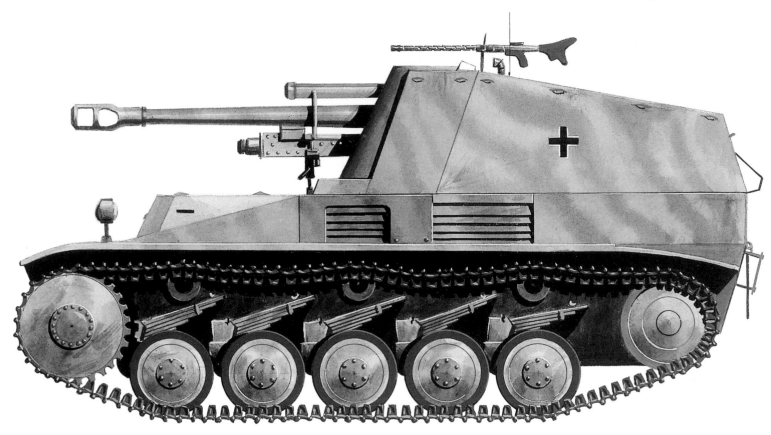

The Panzer III/IV chassis was seen by the German army ordnance department as a suitable mount for a 105mm (4.1in) gun in early 1942. But when the gun was found to work satisfactorily on a Panzer II chassis, all Panzer II production was turned over to the new vehicle: a light field howitzer on a Panzer II chassis. It was given the popular name Wespe (Wasp). One thousand were ordered as an interim measure in February 1943, but this number was reduced to 835 later that year. The Wespe's superstructure had room for a respectable 32 rounds of ammunition, but nevertheless 159 were built as specialised munitions carriers able to carry 90 rounds. Compared to the Panzer II, the Wespe was slightly lengthened, with its engine repositioned forward and three, rather than four, return rollers in the suspension. The driver sat in an enclosed position at the front of the vehicle, while the rest of the crew travelled in the open-topped fighting compartment which was surrounded by a thin armour shield, good against small arms and shrapnel but not much else. The top of the compartment was open to the elements and enemy hand grenades, mortars etc, but could be defended by a machine-gun that was supplied with each Wespe. The main armament could be used in a direct-fire role, but normally was elevated (up to 42 degrees) to provide indirect support fire. The munitions carrier version was cleverly designed so that the gun from a disabled Wespe could be fitted by field maintenance troops, thus creating a 'new' Wespe. Like many German armoured vehicles, the Wespe was delivered in numbers in time for the 1943 summer offensive on the Eastern Front and made its debut at Kursk. More successful than many heavier self-propelled guns, it was speedy, reliable and popular and as a result, saw service on the Eastern and Western Fronts and in Italy until the end of the war.

Specification

Country of Origin:	Germany
Main Armament:	One 105mm (4.1in) leFH18 howitzer
Secondary Armament:	One 7.92mm (0.3in) MG 34 machine-gun carried internally
Combat Weight:	11 tons
Length:	4.81m (15ft 7in)
Width:	2.28m (7ft 6in)
Height:	2.30m (7ft 6in)
Road Speed:	40km/h (25mph)
Road Range:	220 km (138mls)
Crew:	Five

Panzerjäger IV Nashorn Tank Destroyer

The 88mm PaK 43 dual anti-tank/anti-aircraft gun was one of the best all-round weapons of the war, but it was hardly mobile. The invasion of the Soviet Union required artillery that could keep up with the rapid advance. The first successful attempt to self-propel the 'eighty-eight' was the SdKfz 164 Panzerjäger (tank-hunter) IV, based on the Panzer IV chassis. It was regarded as an 'interim' vehicle until new purpose-designed panzerjägers could come along, but was kept in production almost to the end of the war. Known unofficially as the Nashorn (rhinoceros), but officially as the Hornisse (hornet), it featured a new, lightly armoured superstructure in place

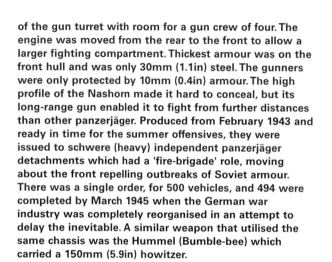

of the gun turret with room for a gun crew of four. The engine was moved from the rear to the front to allow a larger fighting compartment. Thickest armour was on the front hull and was only 30mm (1.1in) steel. The gunners were only protected by 10mm (0.4in) armour. The high profile of the Nashorn made it hard to conceal, but its long-range gun enabled it to fight from further distances than other panzerjäger. Produced from February 1943 and ready in time for the summer offensives, they were issued to schwere (heavy) independent panzerjäger detachments which had a 'fire-brigade' role, moving about the front repelling outbreaks of Soviet armour. There was a single order, for 500 vehicles, and 494 were completed by March 1945 when the German war industry was completely reorganised in an attempt to delay the inevitable. A similar weapon that utilised the same chassis was the Hummel (Bumble-bee) which carried a 150mm (5.9in) howitzer.

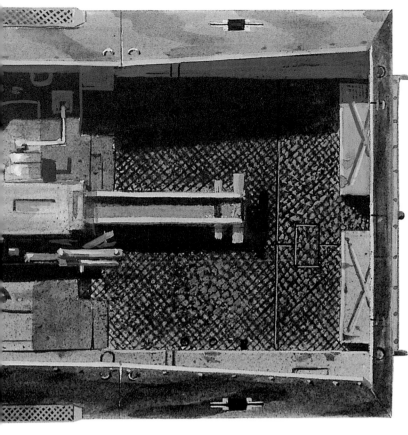

Specification

Country of Origin:	Germany
Main Armament:	One 88mm (3.5in) PaK 43/1 cannon
Secondary Armament:	One 7.92mm (0.3in) MG 34 machine-gun carried internally
Combat Weight:	24 tons
Length:	8.44m (27ft 8in)
Width:	2.86m (9ft 5in)
Height:	2.65m (8ft 8in)
Road Speed:	42km/h (26mph)
Road Range:	215km (133mls)
Crew:	Four

Panzerjäger Tiger (P) Elefant Tank Destroyer

The Elefant tank destroyer fell between earlier lightly armoured 'lash-up' designs such as the Nashorn and the successful Panther-based Jagdpanther. Based on the Porsche Tiger design (and initially known as Ferdinand after Ferdinand Porsche) the Elefant was one of the first German vehicles to carry the long-barrelled 88mm (3.5in) flak gun. The full designation of this gun was the PaK 43/2 L/71; the later part indicating that it was 71 calibres long (the bore was a 71st part of the barrel length). The hull structure of the Ferdinand was basically the same as that of the Porsche Tiger but with 100mm (3.9in) plates bolted to the front, giving a total of 200mm (7.8in) frontal armour protection. The Elefant had twin Maybach engines and a large number of electrical components including an electric gearbox and steering through twin electric motors, all of which contributed to the complexity – and unreliability – of this tank destroyer. In February 1943 Hitler ordered that 90 of these vehicles, given the ordnance number SdKfz 184, be produced and delivered to the front as soon as possible. By abbreviating the test programme, this was achieved by the end of May 1943, in time for the spring offensive on the Eastern Front. Many of the Elefants produced fought at Kursk where they were able to defeat all types of Soviet tank, but they lacked cross-country mobility, were prone to breakdowns and, with no secondary armament, were vulnerable to infantry armed with magnetic mines and other charges. An escort of panzergrenadiers was deemed essential for close-range defence. In late 1943, the surviving 48 vehicles were rebuilt at the factory and were fitted with a bow MG 34 machine-gun for self-defence, a commander's cupola and Zimmerit anti-magnetic coating. Many of these saw service on the Italian front, but proved unsuitable to the poor road conditions and suffered from a lack of spare parts. Most were eventually abandoned or destroyed by their crews.

Specification

Country of Origin:	Germany
Main Armament:	88mm (3.5in) PaK 43/2 cannon
Secondary Armament:	None
Combat Weight:	29 tons
Length:	8.13m (26ft 8in)
Width:	3.38m (11ft 1in)
Height:	2.98m (9ft 10in)
Road Speed:	20km/h (12.5mph)
Road Range:	153km (95mls)
Crew:	Six

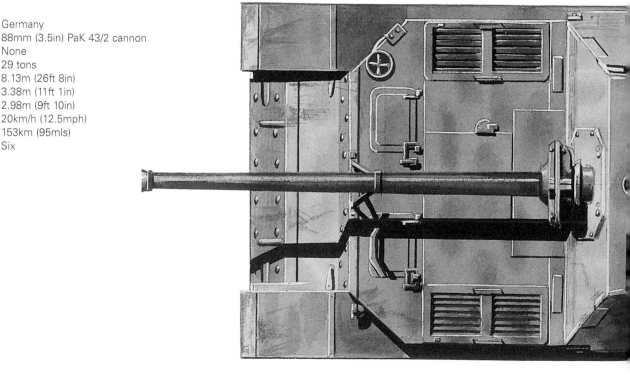

Panzer V Ausf G Medium Heavy Tank

Although it had a disastrous combat debut, the Panther matured to become the best all-round German tank of the war. Conceived as a response to the Russian T-34, the Panther featured sloped frontal armour, wide tracks, a powerful engine and a good gun. As a result, it had good mobility, especially on rough terrain, and was available in large enough numbers to make a difference in many battles. The three new features that the Panther embodied, based on Soviet practice, were large road wheels, sloped armour on all surfaces, and an overhanging gun. This latter feature had been avoided on previous panzers as too restrictive of turret movement. The first prototype was ready in September 1942 and was immediately ordered with a top priority rating: the first production model rolled out only two months later. Several factories were put to work and reached a peak of 330 vehicles per month during 1944. The summer offensive in the Soviet Union was put off until July so that enough Panthers would be ready. In the event, the Panther's rapid development had left many 'bugs' in the first machines that fought at Kursk. Suspensions broke, tracks failed and the engines had a worrying tendency to catch fire. The improved Panther Ausf G (illustrated) which was built from March 1944 rectified most of the deficiencies and also featured a new type glacis plate with a ball-mounted machine-gun, improved crew vision devices and thicker side armour. Some late vehicles had all-steel road wheels (which saved rubber as well as being stronger) and a number had an early infrared sighting device, technology that was well ahead of its time. The Panther comprised half the strength of the panzer divisions by mid-1944 and was active on all fronts. About 450 took part in the Ardennes offensive in late-1944, some disguised as American tank destroyers in an effort to sow confusion in Allied ranks. Total production was 5976 Panthers, 3126 of which were Ausf Gs.

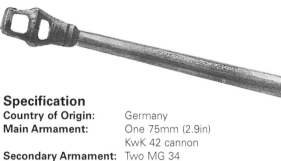

Specification

Country of Origin:	Germany
Main Armament:	One 75mm (2.9in) KwK 42 cannon
Secondary Armament:	Two MG 34 7.92mm (0.3in) machine-guns (one co-axial, one hull-mounted)
Combat Weight:	45.5 tons
Length:	8.86m (29ft)
Width:	3.4m (11ft 2in)
Height:	2.98m (9ft 9in)
Road Speed:	46km/h (29mph)
Road Range:	200km (124mls)
Crew:	Five

Jagdpanzer IV/70 Tank Destroyer

When production of StuG III assault guns was halted by bombing of the Alkett factory in late 1943, Hitler ordered that the StuG superstructure be fitted to the Panzer IV chassis. This configuration had previously been trialled, but not adopted due to other demands on Panzer IV production. At the same time Vomag, one of the Panzer IV constructors, presented their own design for a tank destroyer based on this chassis. Both vehicles were accepted for production, as the StuG IV and the Jagdpanzer IV respectively. The Jagdpanzer IV featured a new superstructure with sloping surfaces and periscopes for crew vision and the vehicle had few excrescences or weaknesses in its ballistic shape. The original main weapon was a 75mm (2.9in) PaK 39 with a barrel 48 calibres long and this was supported by two front-mounted machine-guns. The improved version, the Jagdpanzer IV/70, had a 70-calibre version of the same main gun which gave increased muzzle velocity and thus armour penetration. Front armour was increased to 80mm (3.1in) and this combined with the long gun made the Jagdpanzer IV/70 extremely nose heavy, which caused many failures of the rubber-tyred road

wheels. New steel wheels were fitted on the first two stations to remedy this problem. Most of these tank hunters were equipped with Schürzen or armoured skirts which protected the vulnerable running gear. When Alkett's production lines were running again they were turned over to making Jagdpanzer IV/70s. Their version had a vertical base to the superstructure and was nearly three tons heavier but was otherwise very similar. The basic Jagdpanzer IV was a well-liked and effective tank destroyer which knocked out many Soviet tanks between 1944 and 1945. The big gun, which was installed on Hitler's orders, helped ruin the cross-country handling and slow down the later-model Jagdpanzer IVs. By the time they were in action all combat was defensive and these attributes mattered little any more.

Specification

Country of Origin:	Germany
Main Armament:	One 75mm (2.9in) PaK 42 cannon
Secondary Armament:	One co-axial MG 34 7.92mm (0.3in) machine-gun
Combat Weight:	25.8 tons
Length:	8.5m (27ft 11in)
Width:	3.17m (10ft 5in)
Height:	1.85m (6ft 1in)
Road Speed:	35km/h (22mph)
Road Range:	210km (130mls)
Crew:	Four

SdKfz 173 Jagdpanther Heavy Tank Destroyer

The Jagdpanther was one of the most effective tank destroyers built during World War II although it never appeared on the battlefield in large enough numbers to be decisive. Building on the experience of earlier tank destroyers such as the Ferdinand and the Nashorn, which were by and large makeshift adaptations of obsolete chassis, the Jagdpanther was designed in 1943 to make use of the best chassis available: that of the Panther heavy tank. The result, first demonstrated to Hitler in October 1943, was an unaltered Panther chassis and running gear to which was added a new sloped-front superstructure housing a PaK 43 88mm (3.5in) anti-tank gun in a limited-traverse mount. Frontal armour was 80mm (3.1in) steel and that on the sides 60mm (2.3in) while that on the gun mantlet was a massive 120mm (4.7in). Side skirts were often added in service. Initially designated Panzerjäger Panther, on Hitler's orders it was redesignated Jagdpanther (hunting panther) in February 1944. Production began in that

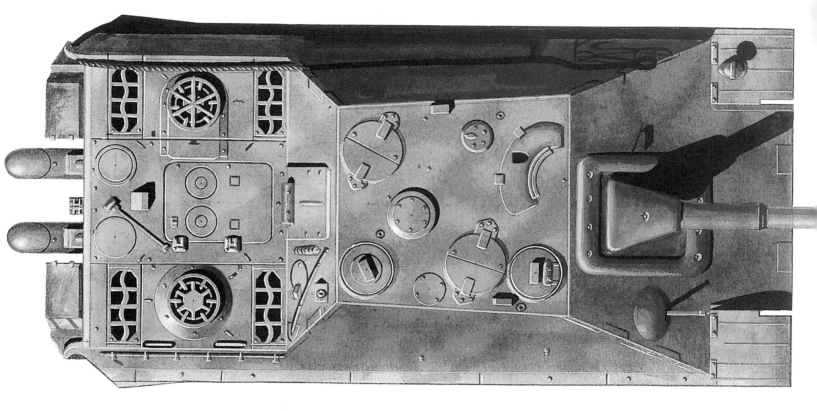

month using the then current production model, the Panther Ausf G as the basis, but with a stronger gearbox originally intended for the unbuilt Panther II. Service entry was in June 1944 with the 559th and 654th Panzerjäger battalions, although the former only ever received enough vehicles to equip one company. Production and delivery problems caused by Allied bombing of factories and railways meant that there were few occasions when the Jagdpanthers were able to concentrate in strength. An exception was the 'Battle of the Bulge' in December 1944 when they proved superior to any opposition, knocking out Allied tanks on a scale out of all proportion to their numbers. However, each Jagdpanther lost was an asset that could not be replaced, as the factories were overrun. Production ceased in April 1945 with the 382nd vehicle and the last Jagdpanthers fought on until they were knocked out or until fuel supplies dried up.

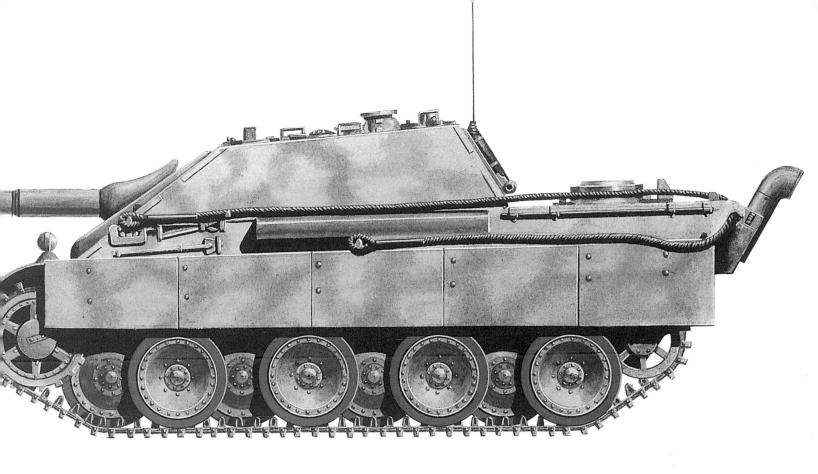

Specification

Country of Origin: Germany
Main Armament: One 88mm (3.5in) PaK 43/4 cannon
Secondary Armament: One hull-mounted 7.92mm (0.3in) MG 34 machine-gun
Combat Weight: 46 tons
Length: 9.9m (32ft 5in)
Width: 3.42m (11ft 2in)
Height: 2.72m (8ft 11in)
Road Speed: 46km/h (29mph)
Road Range: 160km (100mls)
Crew: Five

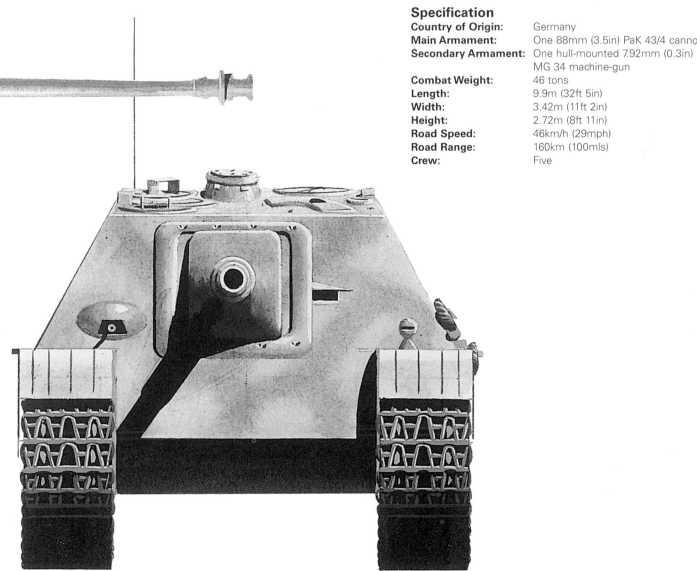

Jadgdpanzer 38(t) Hetzer Tank-destroyer

Specification

Country of Origin:	Germany
Main Armament:	One 75mm (2.9in) PaK 39 cannon
Secondary Armament:	One roof-mounted 7.92mm (0.3in) MG 34 or MG 42 machine-gun
Combat Weight:	15.8 tons
Overall length:	6.20m (20ft 4in)
Hull length:	4.8m (15ft 9in)
Width:	2.50m (8ft 2in)
Height:	2.10m (6ft 11in)
Road Speed:	39km/h (24mph)
Road Range:	250km (155mls)
Crew:	Four

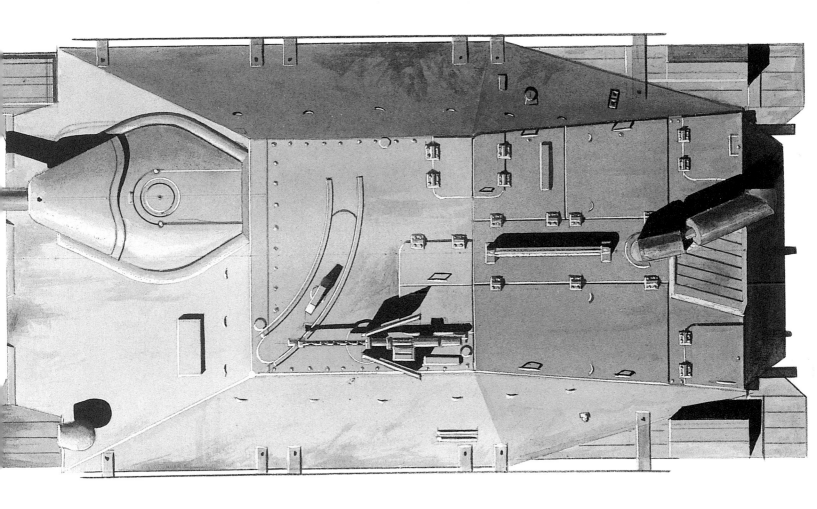

A compact design, little taller than a man, the SdKfz 138/2 Hetzer was an effective tank hunter design in a small package and was a better use of resources than most of the larger German Jadgdpanzer vehicles. When the Germans took over the Czech Skoda and Praga tank factories they initially concentrated on producing the Czech-designed Panzer 38(t), but by 1943 this design was obsolete and a new design was sought to make use of the large Czech tank-building capacity. General Guderian, at that time Inspector of Armoured Units, called for a light tank destroyer with a low silhouette to replace the existing towed and light self-propelled anti-tank guns, and the Panzer 38(t) was a suitable basis for a new vehicle that could be produced rapidly. After trials of a prototype in December 1943, production commenced at a number of Czech plants in April 1944 and the first tank-hunter battalions began to be equipped in July 1944. Hetzer translates as 'baiter' as in someone who goads a bull or bear to attack, and the Jagdpanzer 38(t) used its stealth to pick at formations of much larger Allied tanks before retreating. Its 75mm (2.9in) gun was effective against the armour of most of its opponents. Reports from the front line were very favourable and production was stepped up towards a hoped-for 1000 per month, but the overrunning of the factories in May 1945 saw deliveries cease at (a still respectable) 1577 examples. The Hetzer was very cramped for the four-man crew, a situation slightly relieved on 100 vehicles that had no recoil mechanism as such for the main gun, recoil being absorbed by the vehicle itself. The gun had limited traverse (five degrees to the left and 11 to the right) and elevation (12 degrees up, six degrees down). Secondary armament was limited to a single machine-gun, which was mounted on the roof and controlled remotely from the inside. Armour was light with a maximum of 60mm (2.3in) thickness, but this was made up for by the difficulty in seeing and hitting the diminutive vehicle. After the war, production was restarted for the Czech army and nearly 160 were exported to Switzerland, where they served into the 1970s.

Flakpanzer IV Wirbelwind Anti-aircraft Tank

The Wirbelwind (whirlwind) was the German answer to the increasing threat posed to German armoured columns by the Allied fighter-bombers. Most earlier self-propelled anti-aircraft mounts had single or twin 20mm (0.7in) armament and little armour protection for the crew. The Flakpanzer IV was designed to correct both these deficiencies by having a four-barrelled 20mm (0.7in) weapon in a fully enclosed open-topped turret. The turret was based on the proven Panzer IV Ausf J chassis which allowed it to be integrated into the anti-aircraft platoons of the panzer regiments with little difficulty. The Wirbelwind retained the bow-mounted machine-gun of the Panzer IV and, with the main gun unit able to depress to -10 degree elevation, it had a certain anti-personnel capability in addition to its primary use. All of these vehicles were conversions rather than new-builds, and only 86 were produced, beginning in July 1944. Two inherent problems with the design were the thin (16mm/0.6in) armour plate on the turret and the hand-traversed turret mechanism. By the autumn of 1944, the 20mm (0.7in) Flak 38 was found to be less effective than the 37mm (1.5in) Flak 43 and production of Wirbelwinds was halted in favour of the Ostwind (east wind), a very similar vehicle with the single-barrel 37mm (1.5in) gun.

Specification

Country of Origin:	Germany
Main Armament:	One four-barrelled Flakvierling 38 20mm (0.7in) cannon
Secondary Armament:	One 7.92mm (0.3in) MG 34 machine-gun
Combat Weight:	22 tons
Length:	5.92m (19ft)
Width:	2.9m (9ft 6in)
Height:	2.76m (9ft 1in)
Road Speed:	38km/h (24mph)
Road Range:	200km (124mls)
Crew:	Five

Panzer VI King Tiger Heavy Tank

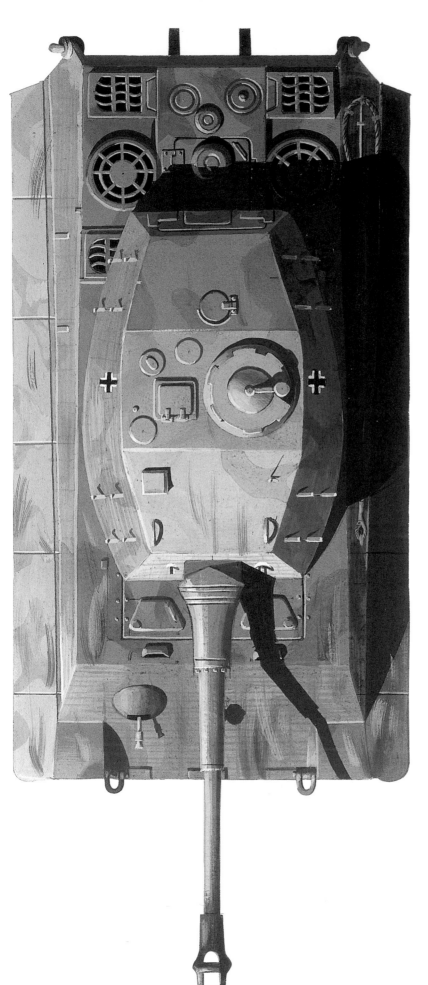

The Tiger II was the largest conventional tank to see service in World War II, only outweighed by its sibling, the Jagdtiger. Its armour and armament were superior to any Allied tank, but it was produced too late and in insufficient quantities to have any effect on the outcome of the war. The best available version of the 88mm (3.5in) gun, the 71-calibre KwK 43, had proved impossible to shoehorn into the Tiger I, so a new tank was ordered that could carry it, at the same time having better armour protection than previous tanks and dominating the battlefield with its size. Hitler was an advocate of 'biggest is best' and took an increasing role in tank design as the war progressed. Projects such as the Tiger II, also known as the Königstiger (King Tiger or Royal Tiger), and the 188-ton 'Maus' were exactly what he liked, and quickly got the go-ahead despite their impracticality and poor use of resources. The Tiger II shared no major components with the Tiger I and in fact was more like a scaled-up Panther in some respects. The first 50 had a Porsche-designed turret which was disliked because of the shot trap it presented. Subsequent vehicles had a Henschel turret with a massive 180mm (7in) of armour on the front face, and the front of the hull was nearly as strong at 150mm (5.9in). The Henschel factory turned out 489 Tiger IIs between January 1944 and March 1945. For once, the new tank was not rushed to the front but first went to training units, although this meant that combat units were not fully equipped until after the Normandy landings. The majority went to independent tank detachments of the army and the SS and caused quite a stir in the Ardennes campaign before they ran out of fuel. The same fate befell most of these giant tanks: at least those that were not abandoned after breaking down, victims of their own complexity. Some were destroyed by air attack, but few, it has to be said, by other tanks.

Specification

Country of Origin:	Germany
Main Armament:	One 88mm (3.5in) KwK 43 cannon
Secondary Armament:	Three 7.92mm (0.3in) MG 34 machine-guns (one co-axial, one in hull, one on turret roof)
Combat Weight:	68 tons
Length:	10.3m (33ft 11in)
Width:	3.76m (12ft 4in)
Height:	3.08m (10ft 1in)
Road Speed:	35km/h (22mph)
Road Range:	170km (105mls)
Crew:	Five

Jagdpanzer VI Jagdtiger Heavy Tank Destroyer

Specification

Country of Origin:	Germany
Main Armament:	One 128mm (5in) PaK 44 cannon
Secondary Armament	One 7.92mm (0.3in) MG 34 and one 7.92mm (0.3in) MG 42 machine-gun
Combat Weight:	70 tons
Length:	10.65m (34ft 11in)
Width:	3.63m (11ft 11in)
Height:	2.95m (9ft 8in)
Road Speed:	38km/h (24mph)
Road Range:	170km (106mls)
Crew:	Six

The Jagdtiger (hunting tiger) was the heaviest AFV to enter service during World War II and carried the second-largest gun of any wartime tank or tank destroyer. The 128mm (5in) gun was designed as an anti-tank gun. It could theoretically defeat 148mm (5.8in) armour at 2000m (2187yds), which meant any tank in the world at a slightly lesser distance. The Jagdtiger's own upper frontal armour was a record 250mm (9.8in) which was impenetrable by anything short of a battleship. It was developed, as was the practice of the time, as the tank destroyer counterpart to the latest battle tank, the Tiger II or King Tiger. The design received Hitler's personal approval in October 1943 and a prototype was ready in April 1944. Orders were that after 150 were completed, production was to be halted in favour of Panthers, but this was reversed and production restarted with all haste in January 1945.

In fact, only 77 were ever delivered due to disruption caused by bombing, which also affected gun production. It is thought that some Jagdtigers were delivered with relatively puny 88mm (3.5in) guns. The two units that received Jagdtigers – one panzerjäger battalion and one independent heavy tank battalion – fought on the Western Front, the former in the Ardennes counter-offensive of December 1944, and the latter in defence of Germany, including at the Remagen Bridge in March 1945. With the same powerplant as much smaller tanks and its enormous weight, the Jagdtiger was fuel-thirsty, unmanoeuvrable, slow and just about impossible to conceal. Two gun loaders helped keep the rate of fire up, but eventually most were overwhelmed by infantry with bazookas or charges that struck at the most vulnerable parts, the wheels and tracks, and they became mileposts on the road to Berlin.

Sturmmörser Tiger Assault Mortar Tank

The Sturmmörser (assault mortar) Tiger or Sturm Tiger was an extraordinary conversion of the Tiger I tank to fire a heavy rocket-assisted projectile against fixed targets. It could operate in the direct assault role or provide indirect fire at ranges of up to 6km (3.7mls). The 380mm (14.9in) mortar itself was originally a naval design intended for use by U-boats against land targets, and could be seen as an ancestor of the ballistic missiles on today's submarines. When the Kriegsmarine dropped the idea, it was taken up as a land-based weapon, and the only suitable carriage for it was the Tiger tank. Troops on the Eastern Front had requested such a weapon (of perhaps 210mm/8.2in) for engaging difficult targets with indirect fire and to keep up with a mobile front line. The Sturm Tiger promised this and more, but by the time production was underway in August 1944, Germany was on the defensive and only a small number were ordered. Alkett made the conversion using Tiger Ausf Es as the basis, upon which was added a new box-like superstructure with a sloped front. The ball-mounted Raketenwerfer (rocket projector) was mounted slightly off-centre and had a series of holes around its rim for venting rocket gases. Only 12 of the projectiles could be stowed inside, but others could be lifted off a supply vehicle with the built-in hand-operated crane system mounted at the rear of the superstructure and lowered through a large roof hatch. Handling the shells, which weighed 350kg (761lb) each was a delicate and dangerous business and another winch system was installed inside to move the shells from their racks to the breech of the projector. Sources vary as to the number produced as being between 10 and 81, but a likely figure is 18. They were issued to three different Sturmmörser companies and their giant mortars found some role in the defence of Germany rather than their intended purpose of blowing apart enemy strongpoints with a single shot.

Specification

Country of Origin: Germany
Main Armament: One 380mm (14.9in) StuM RW 61 rocket mortar
Secondary Armament: One hull-mounted MG 34 7.92mm (0.3in) machine-gun
Combat Weight: 65 tons
Length: 6.28m (20ft 7in)
Width: 3.57m (11ft 4in)
Height: 2.85m (9ft 4in)
Road Speed: 40km/h (25mph)
Road Range: 120km (75mls)
Crew: Seven

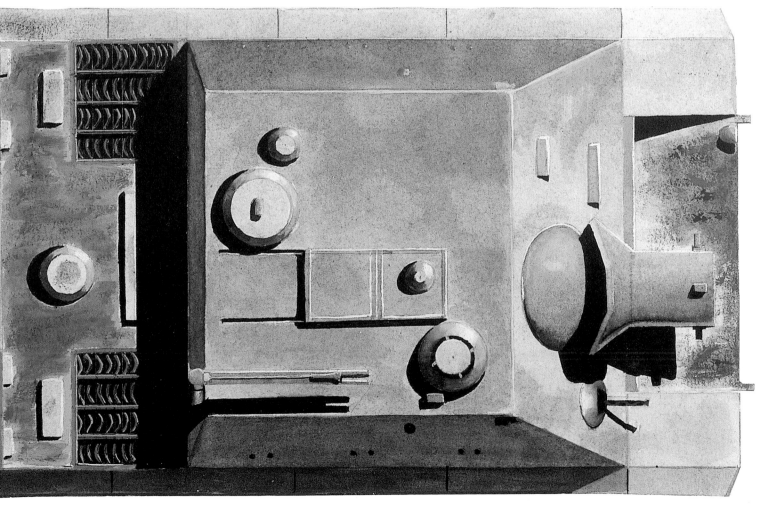

M3 Stuart Light Tank

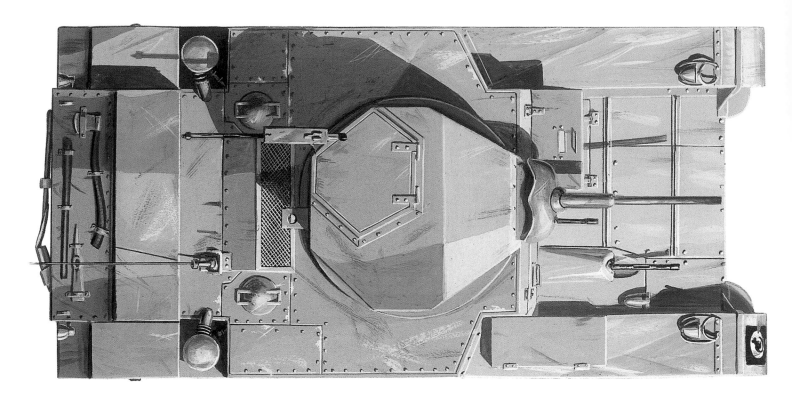

Developed from a series of light tanks (initially called 'combat cars') produced in the 1930s, the M3 was the main tank type in service with the United States Army at the outbreak of war. The M3 had increased armour especially on frontal areas compared to its predecessors, a stronger suspension with larger trailing idler wheel and no vision ports in the turret. Most of these improvements came about in light of combat reports from Europe between 1939 and 1940. The M3 was approved for production in July 1940 and this began in March 1941 when previous contracts had been completed. Initial versions had a riveted turret as well as hull armour, but this was soon replaced by a cast armour turret because of the tendency of rivets to 'pop' when the tank was hit. The initial M3 version had a pair of machine-guns in the sponsons for operation by the driver, but these were often removed as seen here. M3s were sent to Britain under Lend-lease as soon as they became available and were available in strength for battles in the Western desert by November 1941. They proved a useful addition to British tank strength throughout the desert war although they were short on range, a deficiency partly remedied by adding auxiliary fuel tanks on later models. The official British name for the M3 was General Stuart, usually abbreviated to Stuart, but they were also known unofficially as Honeys. The standard engine was a seven-cylinder Continental petrol unit, but many of the early M3s were supplied with a nine-cylinder Guiberson diesel without change of designation. This caused logistic problems, especially for the British, who named the latter version Stuart II. The M3 – and the later welded-hull M3A1 and M3A3 versions – were soon outclassed in tank versus tank combat but proved useful in reconnaissance units and in theatres such as China and Burma where their small size was an asset on rough jungle trails. The US Army declared the M3 series obsolete in July 1943, having introduced the larger M5, but the British and other users continued operating Stuarts until the end of the war and well after in some cases.

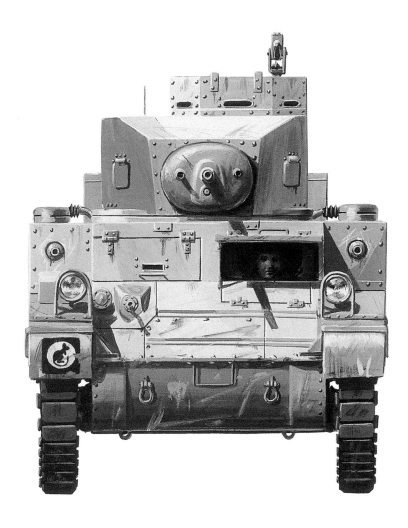

Specification

Country of Origin:	USA
Main Armament:	One M5 37mm (1.5in) cannon
Secondary Armament:	Five 7.6mm (0.3in) machine-guns (one co-axial, one in forward hull, one on turret roof and two in side sponsons)
Combat Weight:	11.2 tons
Length:	4.54m (14ft 11in)
Width:	2.23m (7ft 4in)
Height:	2.51m (8ft 3in)
Road Speed:	58km/h (36mph)
Road Range:	112km (70mls)
Crew:	Four

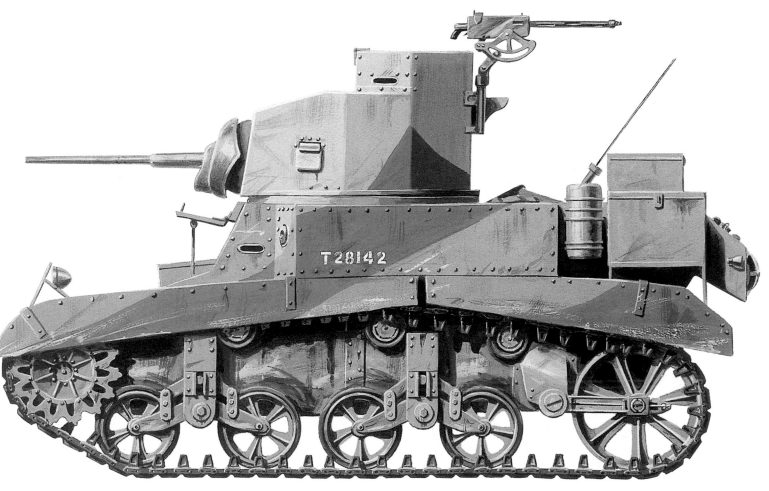

M3 Lee Medium Tank

In 1940, the largest gun mounted on an American tank was of only 37mm (1.5in) calibre. At the same time German tanks with 75mm (2.9in) guns were cutting a swathe through the armoured units of Great Britain and France, which were also mostly equipped with 37mm (1.5in) gun tanks. The US Army's Chief of Infantry demanded that US medium tanks carry 75mm (2.9in) guns, but the only suitable vehicle, the M2A1 which carried eight machine-guns in its superstructure, could not mount such a gun in its small turret. A stopgap solution was to mount the 75mm (2.9in) gun in the right side of the hull and retain the 37mm (1.5in) turret on top. The result was the M3 medium tank, which was designed, developed and put into production with astonishing haste. By August 1941, production had begun at three plants, one of which had been built from scratch. A further two plants produced M3s to an initial British order of 500. These British vehicles had a contoured cast turret with no cupola, giving a lower profile, and were named Grant Is (after US General Ulysses S. Grant). These tanks were of critical importance at the Battle of Gazala in May 1942, being the first British tanks able to outgun the German panzers. The main gun, which was a development of a World War I French weapon, was appreciated for its dual-purpose capability, able to fire armour-piercing (AP) rounds against tanks and high explosive (HE) shots in the infantry support role. The configuration of the tank, which needed to be turned bodily towards the target to engage it with the main gun, was a tactical disadvantage, as was the high profile and the riveted and welded armour. The vehicle illustrated is an early-production M3 (which the British named Lee after Grant's opponent in the Civil War) with a riveted hull and large side doors. Later models featured cast hulls, gyro-stabilisation for the guns and power traverse for the turret. The running gear of the M3 Lee/Grant became the basis for many other vehicles, including (in modified form) the M4 Sherman series. In December 1942, the last of 6258 M3 series vehicles was delivered and by April 1944 the tank was declared obsolete.

Specification

Country of Origin: USA

Main Armament: One M3 75mm (2.9in) howitzer, one M5 37mm (1.5in) cannon

Secondary Armament: Four 7.6mm (0.3in) machine-guns (one in upper turret, one co-axial in main turret, two hull-mounted)

Combat Weight: 27.2 tons

Length: 5.63m (18ft 6in)

Width: 2.7m (8ft 11in)

Height: 3.12m (10ft 3in)

Road Speed: 42km/h (26mph)

Road Range: 190km (120mls)

Crew: Six

LVT-4 Tracked Landing Vehicle

The LVT-4 evolved from the earlier tracked landing vehicles LVT-1, -2 and -3 which in turn were descendants of the Alligator, a 1930s lightweight tracked amphibious vehicle designed by engineer Donald Roebling for rescue work in the Florida Everglades. The US Marine Corps took an interest in the concept after an article on the vehicle was published in a 1937 *Life* magazine and, following trials and modifications, ordered 300 LVT (Landing Vehicle, Tracked) 1s as ship-to-shore cargo carriers. Actual construction of the Alligators was undertaken by the Ford Machinery Company (FMC) in California. The LVT-2 was a revised and improved model with the engine and drivetrain of the M2 light tank, but its central cargo compartment was hard to load and unload and was bisected by the driveshaft, restricting its use to troops and small items. FMC addressed these problems on the LVT-4 which had the engine moved forward to behind the drivers' compartment and a rear ramp fitted. This allowed much easier loading and safer disembarking under fire and for the carriage of wheeled equipment such as Jeeps and light artillery pieces. The first LVT-4 Water Buffalo was delivered at the end of 1943, followed by 8350 others, making it the most numerous of all the AMTRACs (amphibious tractors) produced. The majority of these vehicles went to the US Army who were preparing for the Normandy invasion, but in the end those few that were used in Europe were mainly used by the British or for river crossings rather than beach invasions. In the Pacific, the Marines valued them for their ability to cross coral reefs and carry them inland, things that landing craft could not do. After the bloody Tarawa operation, where many were sunk by shellfire, the need for armour-plated and better-armed versions became apparent.

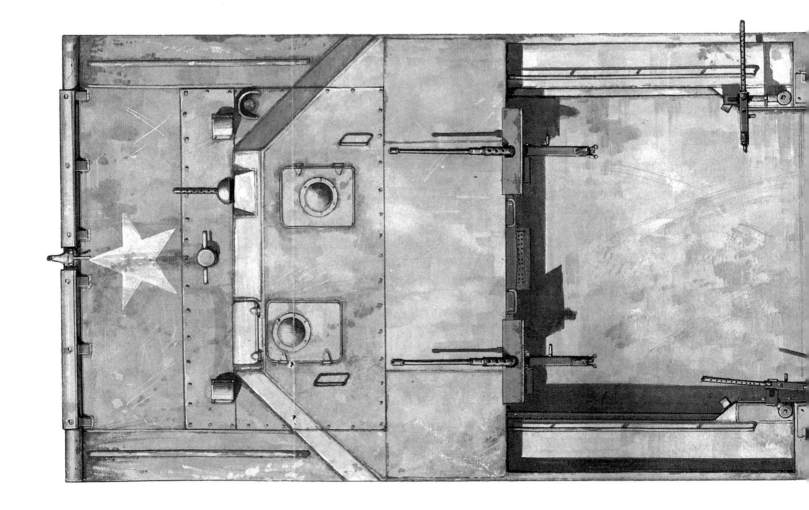

Specification

Country of Origin:	USA
Main Armament:	None
Secondary Armament:	Two 12.5mm (0.5in) machine-guns and three 7.6mm (0.3in) machine-guns
Combat Weight:	15 tons
Length:	8.50m (27ft 10in)
Width:	3.25m (10ft 8in)
Height:	2.64m (8ft 9in)
Road Speed:	32km/h (20mph)
Water Speed:	12km/h (6.5mph)
Road Range:	480km (300mls)
Water Range:	322km (200mls)
Crew:	Two

T17E1 Staghound I Light Armoured Car

The Staghound was an American design for a heavy 'armored' car that was never used by US forces, all production going to Britain and its Commonwealth allies. The US Army had seen the use the Desert Rats had made of armoured cars in the Western Desert and had two vehicles built, the Ford T17 6x6 (six wheels, six-wheel drive) and the Chevrolet T17E1 4x4. The British saw the potential of this latter vehicle and ordered an initial 300, although the Americans themselves changed their requirements and concentrated on other avenues of development. By the end of 1942, the first examples were being shipped to Britain where they were issued to British, Canadian, Belgian, Indian and New Zealand units as the Staghound Mk I. The Staghound, with its high speed, good range, thick armour and hydraulically-traversed turret, was a popular and effective weapon. With twin six-cylinder 72kW (97hp) petrol engines and power steering, the Staghound was powerful and pleasant to drive. It proved adaptable to a number of uses including anti-aircraft (the Staghound AA with twin 12.7mm/0.5in guns) and anti-tank (Staghound Mk III with a Crusader turret and 75mm/2.9in gun). The Staghound Command was a turretless variant with extra radios and machine-guns, used by British armoured car regiments as a command vehicle, usually with the regimental HQ troop. After the war, Staghounds were supplied to various nations including Denmark, India and South Africa, and remained in service for some years with the British army itself.

Specification

Country of Origin:	USA
Main Armament:	One 37mm (1.5in) cannon
Secondary Armament:	Three 7.62mm (0.3in) machine-guns (one hull-mounted, one co-axial, one on turret roof)
Combat Weight:	13.7 tons
Length:	5.49m (18ft)
Width:	2.69m (8ft 10in)
Height:	2.36m (7ft 9in)
Road Speed:	89km/h (55mph)
Road Range:	724km (450mls)
Crew:	Five

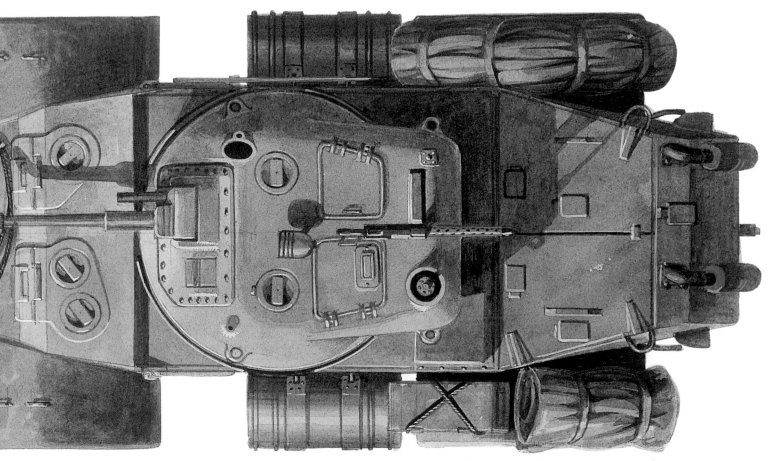

LVT(A)-4 Armoured Tracked Landing Vehicle

Following the near-disaster of the Tarawa invasion when many AMTRACs (amphibious tractors) were lost for the want of close-in fire support, new versions of the LVT Water Buffalo were designed to meet the requirement for a 'floating tank'. The resulting LVT(A)s were essentially the same as the LVTs but built in armour plate rather than mild steel and with one of a variety of tank or gun carriage turrets added on top. The LVT(A)-4 replaced the M5 Stuart turret and 37mm (1.5in) cannon of the LVT(A)-2 with the complete turret of the M8 HMC (Howitzer Motor Carriage) with its 75mm (2.9in) howitzer. A canvas cover protected the open turret when not in action. The turreted versions carried buoyancy bags to compensate for the extra weight. A total of 1890 LVT(A)-4s was built between 1944 and 1945. Some carried rocket launchers at the rear hull and there was a version with an E7 flame projector in place of the howitzer. The so-called 'Marianas model' had three machine-guns added for self defence in preparation for that campaign. One major problem with the LVT(A)-4 was that it was impossible to fire the main gun accurately while bobbing up and down in the waves, especially with hand traverse of the turret. The subsequent LVT(A)-5, which was visually identical to late-model LVT(A)-4s, had a gyro-stabiliser for the turret and power traverse. This was the last of the original AMTANKs, as they had become known, and saw active service in the Korean War. All the LVT series were propelled through the water by the tracks, which had integral cup-shaped grousers. This eliminated the complexity and volume of a propeller and shaft as used on other amphibious vehicles, but resulted in a rather low water speed.

Specification
Country of Origin: USA
Main Armament: M2 or M3 75mm (2.9in) howitzer
Secondary Armament: None on early models
Combat Weight: 18.3 tons
Length: 7.9m (26ft 2in)
Width: 3.25m (10ft 8in)
Height: 2.09m (10ft 3in)
Road Speed: 40km/h (25mph)
Water Speed: 10km/h (6.5mph)
Road Range: 483km (300mls)
Water Range: 322km (200mls)
Crew: Six

M7B1 Priest Howitzer Motor Carriage

The M7 self-propelled howitzers were developed to supply mobile artillery support to the tank divisions equipping with the new M3 medium tanks in 1941. The M3 chassis was roomy enough for a large gun and its crew and would simplify logistics and operations alongside the M3 tanks. It was adapted as the basis for the M7 HMC (Howitzer Motor Carriage) in February 1942. The British ordered a massive 5500 as soon as they saw the pilot model, but priority was for the US Army and only a few could be spared to begin with. Those that were available by the end of 1942 played an important part in the Battle of El Alamein, which saw the defeat of German forces in the desert. The name Priest, which was as usual given by the British, was said to be a reference to the 'pulpit' commander's position. This ecclesiastical theme was taken up for other gun carriages, namely the Sexton and Bishop. The tactical concept of the Priest was to provide heavy artillery support with mainly indirect fire rather than direct assault on enemy positions, therefore the armour that was provided was thin (25mm/0.9in maximum) and good only against small arms fire and shrapnel. The 105mm (4.1in) gun was larger than that on any Allied tank, but comparatively light for such a large hull. A total of 69 rounds of 105mm (4.1in) ammunition could be stowed within the vehicle. The M7B1 was built to the same specifications as the M7, but was based on the M4 Sherman chassis as the M3 was phased out of production by September 1943. The main recognition feature of the two versions was the three-piece nose of the M7 and the smooth cast nose of the M7B1. The M7B1 had two operating crew (a commander and a driver) and a gun crew of five. US versions were used to the end of the war in Northwest Europe, but Sextons replaced British versions early in the Normandy campaign. Redundant Priests in Italy and elsewhere were often divested of their gun and converted to Priest Kangaroo armoured personnel carriers.

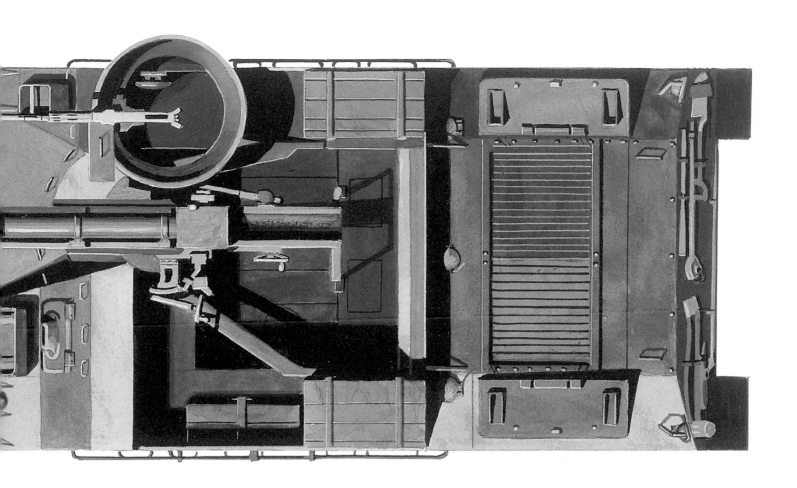

Specification

Country of Origin:	USA
Main Armament:	One M1A2 105mm (4.1in) howitzer
Secondary Armament:	One cupola-mounted 12.6mm (0.5in) calibre machine-gun
Combat Weight:	22.6 tons
Length:	6.20m (20ft 4in)
Width:	2.87m (9ft 5in)
Height:	2.53m (8ft 4in)
Road Speed:	42km/h (26mph)
Road Range:	200km (125mls)
Crew:	Seven

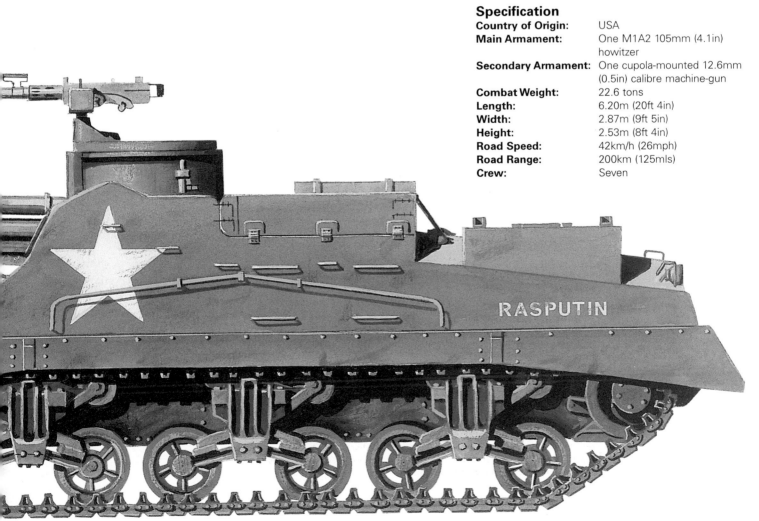

M22 Locust Light Tank (Airborne)

Specifications

Country of Origin:	USA
Main Armament:	One 37mm (1.5in) M6 cannon
Secondary Armament:	One co-axial 7.6mm (0.3in) machine-gun
Combat Weight:	7.4 tons
Length:	3.93m (12ft 11in)
Width:	2.16m (7ft 1in)
Height:	1.82m (6ft 1in)
Road Speed:	64km/h (40mph)
Road Range:	217km (135mls)
Crew:	Three

The M22 was the smallest and lightest American tank of the war and was designed to be air-portable for quick deployment to the battlefield. The US Army Ordnance Department formulated a requirement for a light tank for the airborne forces in May 1941 with input from the US Armored Force and the US Army Air Force (who would have to transport any such tanks). The main design features were lightweight and compact dimensions to enable carriage in the transport aircraft of the period. Marmon-Herrington submitted the most promising design to meet the specification and their T9 pilot model was delivered in the autumn of 1941. Despite a main armament of only 37mm (1.5in) calibre and a maximum armour thickness of 25mm (0.9in) the T9 was deemed too heavy and non-essential fittings such as power turret traverse and gun gyro-stabiliser were removed. The revised T9E1 model was accepted and 830 were built, starting in March 1943. It was accepted into US service as the M22 in September 1944 but never saw combat with American forces, partly because they had no gliders large enough to carry it. The only method of air transport was to attach it beneath modified C-54 transports with the turret removed and stored inside, thus reducing its tactical utility. Four large brackets on the hull were fitted for attaching the tank to the aircraft. Large numbers of M22s were supplied to Great Britain who named it Locust. The British had developed the Hamilcar glider to carry their own Tetrarch light tank and this aircraft proved capable of carrying the Locust as well. They saw action only once when a small number were landed by Hamilcar to take part in the Rhine crossing operation on 24 March 1945. Despite its high speed and low footprint, the Locust suffered from the compromises needed for airborne carriage, namely its small gun and thin armour.

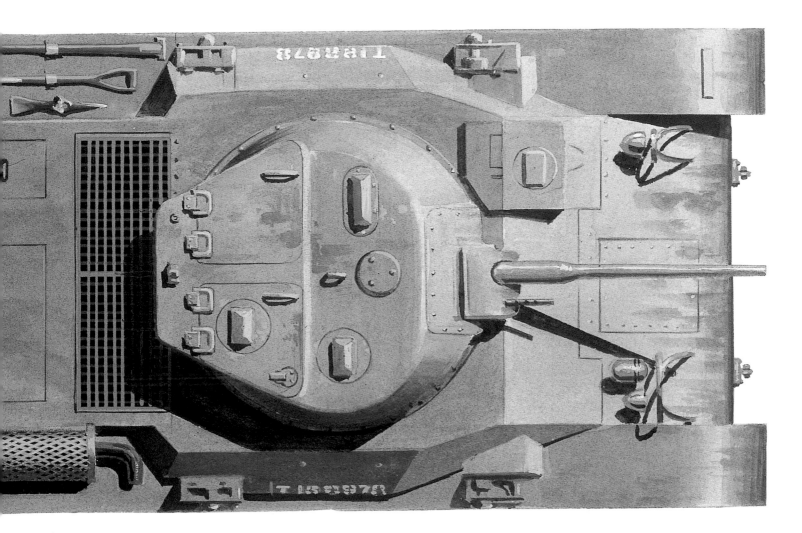

M24 Chaffee Light Tank

In 1939 most light tanks (i.e. almost all tanks) were equipped
with main armament in the 37mm to 40mm (1.5in to 1.57in) class.
By 1942 it was recognised that this was now inadequate to defeat
the armour of even other light tanks and efforts were made in the
US and elsewhere to provide smaller tanks with effective
firepower. The M24 was developed by the US Army's Ordnance
Department in conjunction with Cadillac (designers of the M5
light tank) and incorporated a number of features of this earlier
model such as the twin Cadillac V-8 engines and Hydramatic
suspension. The majority of the M24 – including the running gear
and turret – was of completely new design, although the M6
75mm (2.9in) main gun was originally a World War I French
howitzer which had in turn been adapted and lightened (as the
T13E1) for use in the B-25G bomber for anti-shipping use.
Secondary armament was standard for a light tank with two
built-in machine-guns: another pintle-mounted machine-gun for
anti-aircraft defence and a grenade launcher mounted on the
turret. The M24 was designed as part of a 'light combat team' or
family of vehicles using the same chassis including mortar and
AA gun carriages, but most of these projects were cancelled
when the war ended in 1945. Versions that did see service
included the M19 with twin 40mm (1.57in) AA guns and the M37
Howitzer Motor Carriage (HMC). The M24 itself saw relatively little
wartime service although it was rushed into service in Europe in
1945 where its high speed and reliability were appreciated, and
took part in the battle for Okinawa in the Pacific. A small number
of M24s was supplied to the British and they named it Chaffee
after General Adna R. Chaffee, the first commander of the US
Armored Force. Post-war, the M24 saw much service with the US
and its allies and was to become the basis for the M41, M48 and
M60 series of tanks.

Specification

Country of Origin:	USA
Main Armament:	75mm (2.9in) M6 cannon
Secondary Armament:	Two 7.6mm (0.3in) Browning machine-guns (one on hull, one co-axial); one 12.5mm (0.5in) Browning machine-gun on turret roof; one M3 grenade launcher.
Combat Weight:	18.4 tons
Length:	5.48m (18ft)
Width:	2.97m (9ft 8in)
Height:	2.50m (8ft 2in)
Road Speed:	56km/h (35mph)
Road Range:	160km (100mls)
Crew:	Five

Ram Kangaroo Armoured Personnel Carrier

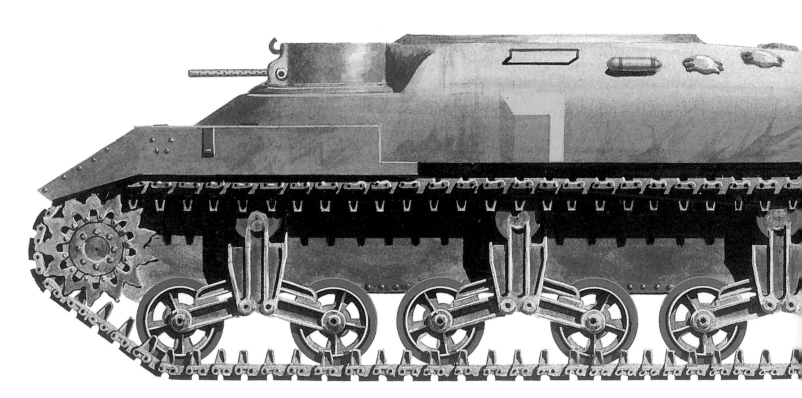

On the outbreak of war in September 1939, Britain looked to the Empire to supply what war material and agricultural supplies it could to supplement its own hard-pressed industries and farms. The only Commonwealth nation with the heavy industrial base to begin armoured vehicle production was Canada and soon railway engineering firms were hard at work producing Valentines for British and Canadian use. A heavier tank was desired and rights were purchased to licence-build the US M3 (Lee/Grant) tank, but it was realised that its sponson-mounted gun arrangement was outmoded and it was decided to adapt the basic chassis and running gear with a locally-designed hull and turret. The result was the Cruiser Tank Ram Mk I mounting a 2pdr (40mm/1.6in) gun, the first of which was rolled out by the Montreal Locomotive Works in June 1941. The name Ram came from the family crest of the head of the Canadian armoured forces. The Ram bore a strong resemblance to the M4 Sherman then under development in the USA, but it seems that similarity was coincidental, both designs being adaptions of the same chassis to the same specification. Production of the Ram Mk II began in late 1941 and soon began to equip Canadian armoured divisions on their way to Europe. As a battle tank, the Ram never saw combat due to the growing availability of the (in a number of respects inferior) Sherman by mid-1943. Instead, the Ram was developed for other purposes including the Sexton SP gun and the Ram Kangaroo, which was one of the first fully tracked armoured personnel carriers (APCs) in use anywhere. The conversion was made by removing the turret and installing rudimentary seating for up to 11 troops in battle order and adding hand-grips on the hull to aid mounting and dismounting. The hull-mounted machine-gun was retained. The Kangaroo was widely used by the armoured troop carrier battalions of the 79th Armoured Division in Northwest Europe and by the British army for some years after the war. A related version was the Wallaby, an ammunition carrier for the Sexton.

Specification

Country of Origin:	Canada
Main Armament:	None
Secondary Armament:	One Browning 7.6mm (0.3in) machine-gun
Combat Weight:	29 tons
Length:	5.79m (19ft)
Width:	2.78m (9ft 1in)
Height:	2.47m (8ft 9in) with turret
Road Speed:	40km/h (25mph)
Road Range:	232km (144mls)
Crew:	Two, provision for 11 troops

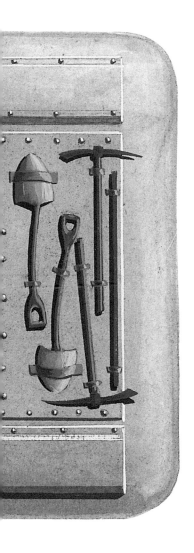

T-35B Heavy Tank

One of the most extraordinary, and heaviest, tanks to be used in the war, the T-35 'land battleship' was inspired by British experimental tanks of the 1920s, the plans of which the Soviets acquired surreptitiously. First displayed at the May Day parade in Moscow in 1933, the prototype T-35 caused a great deal of interest in the West, although no other nation bothered to copy many of its features. The main armament was a 76.2mm (3in) howitzer, the heaviest tank gun seen to that time, backed up with a pair of 37mm (1.5in), later 45mm (1.7in), turrets mounted fore and aft. These were each equivalent to or better than the armament of any Western tank; in fact they were the turrets of

light tanks, from the far more useful BT-5. The T-35 was designated a 'penetration tank' with the role of leading lighter tanks and infantry into the assault and defending itself from all directions in the process. A cynic might say that the rear-facing aft turret had a role in preventing dissent in the ranks following. Given the difficulty of moving the T-35 by rail, and its own limited range, it served with only one unit, the 5th Heavy Tank Brigade whose role was the defence of Moscow. This also allowed T-35s to make their annual appearance at May Day parades in increasing numbers as production (slowly) got underway. Total production was 62 of this model and six more with a conical

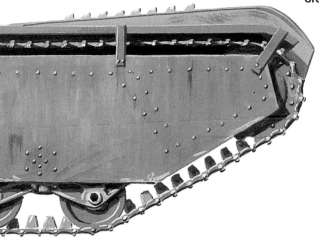

Specification

Country of Origin:	Soviet Union
Main Armament:	One 76.2mm (3in) howitzer
Secondary Armament:	Two 45mm (1.7in) 1934 cannons, four 7.6mm (0.3in) DT machine-guns (one co-axial, two in turrets, one in hull)
Combat Weight:	45 tons
Length:	9.72m (31ft 11in)
Width:	3.20m (10ft 6in)
Height:	3.43m (11ft 4in)
Road Speed:	30km/h (18.6mph)
Road Range:	150km (93mls)
Crew:	Eleven

turret. The T-35 was noted in the Russo-Finnish war and in the winter of 1941 some saw combat outside Moscow where several were captured, having run out of fuel, and at least one was taken to Germany for thorough testing. The tank was unmanoeuverable but less surprisingly, thinly armoured with a maximum thickness of 30mm (1.18in). The crew of 11 was more akin to that of a World War I tank with its members communicating by internal telephone. Tanks like the T-35 had their main effect in convincing the Germans (erroneously) of the backwardness of Russian tank design in the last years of peace.

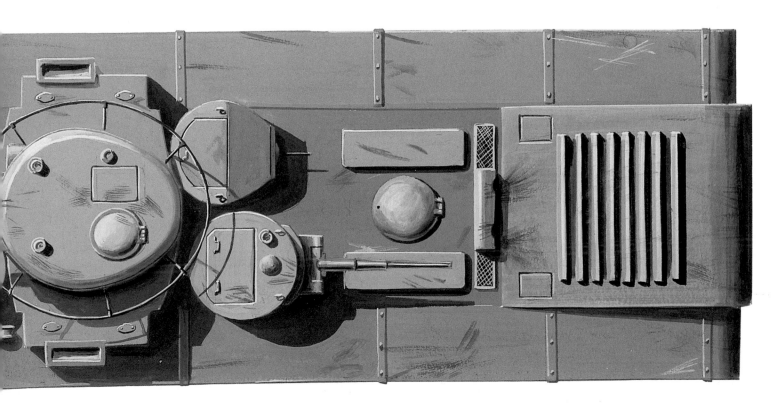

T-34/76A Medium Tank

The T-34 was built in vast quantities barely approached by any other AFV and, while not perfect, had perhaps the best fighting qualities of any tank of the war. Remarkably, the Soviets managed to keep its existence completely secret until the German invasion in June 1941. It was developed by the experimental department of the Kharkov Locomotive Factory as the T-32. This was followed by the T-34 with thicker armour and other improvements. In early 1940 two prototypes of the T-34 were put through gruelling trials and demonstrated in the Kremlin courtyard, where they found favour with the Soviet leadership who soon ordered 220, then 600 units. The Germans were shocked to encounter the T-34 in June 1941, having believed that all Soviet tanks were either lightweights or multi-turreted monsters. The T-34 was fast, well armed, manoeuvrable and its armour was sloped so that its maximum effectiveness was doubled for its thickness. German anti-tank shells just bounced off, unless they struck under the gun mantlet which was an unfortunate 'shot trap'. The gun of the original model, the T34/76A, was a dual-purpose weapon that could fire high explosive and armour-piercing shells and was fitted in a cramped two-man rolled/pressed steel turret. During 1941, a new cast turret was introduced, followed by a long-barrelled gun and another new turret with a commander's cupola. The major change in production after 1943 was the arrival of the 85mm (3.4in) gun T-34/85 which had a new three-man turret and a larger-diameter turret ring. Both the T-34/76 and /85 were built in parallel until mid-1944 when production of the former stopped after 35,099 were completed. The massive losses of T-34s in 1941 and 1943 were due respectively to the speed and surprise of the German advance and the development of new German heavy tanks such as the Tiger and Panther. The T-34/85 redressed this balance and remained the principal Soviet tank until after the war, when it was exported to many communist nations. Total production of all models was over 64,000.

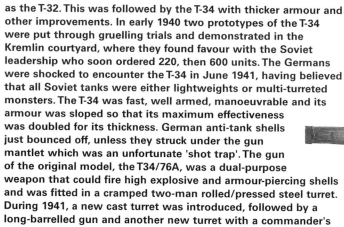

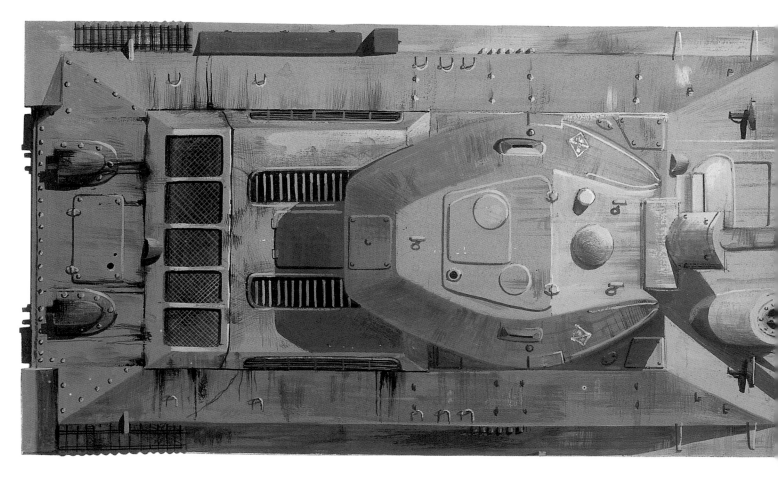

Specification

Country of Origin: Soviet Union
Main Armament: One 76.2mm (3in) 1942 (F34) cannon
Secondary Armament: Two 7.62mm (0.3in) DT machine-guns
(one co-axial, one on hull)
Combat Weight: 30 tons
Length: 5.92m (19ft 5in)
Width: 3m (8ft 10in)
Height: 2.45m (8ft 1in)
Road Speed: 55km/h (34mph)
Road Range: 300km (186mls)
Crew: Four

KV-1A Heavy Tank

In 1938, the Soviets saw the need for a modern heavy tank to replace the obsolete multi-turreted models then in service. Two of the three designs put forward had at least two turrets, but one was of conventional appearance with heavy armour and armament. Two examples of this tank, which was able to carry thicker armour because of the weight saved by having a single turret, were sent to the Finnish front for combat evaluation and proved successful. The tank was accepted as the KV-1, KV standing for Klementy Voroshilov, Marshal of the Soviet Union and pre-war defence commissar. Full-scale production was ordered and 141 of the initial model, the KV-1A, were produced in 1940. In 1941 211 were produced before the German invasion on 22 June, meaning that reasonable numbers of this fine tank were available to be rushed to the front line. What is remarkable is that 900 more were produced that year after the factory was moved bodily to a site east of the Ural Mountains. The Germans had not suspected a Soviet tank with such 'shell-proof' armour, but this advantage was neutralised by the poorly trained Soviet tank crews, who too often got too close to the larger anti-tank guns instead of picking off the enemy from a safe range. The KV-1As

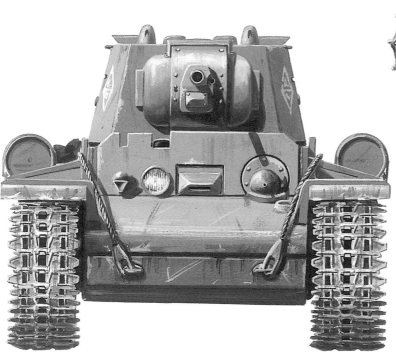

had a high ammunition capacity of up to 114 rounds, which was fortunate as a complex gun sighting system meant that many shots were wasted. Many KV-1As were lost to Stuka dive-bomber attacks and more to minor mechanical problems that could not be fixed before the enemy overran the Soviet positions. During 1940, the original L-11 gun was replaced by the longer-barrelled gun then used on the T-34 and seen in this illustration. Later a heavy new cast turret was added, which slowed the KV-1 down and made it less agile. This prompted one general to (bravely) ask Stalin what the point was of this unmanoeuvrable heavy tank that broke bridges but had only the armament of a medium tank. Some KV-1 models produced in 1942 had an 85mm (3.4in) gun but heavier armour, and thus were half a ton heavier and 6km/h (4mph) slower.

Specification

Country of Origin:	Soviet Union
Main Armament:	One 76.2mm (3in) 1940 (F 34) cannon
Secondary Armament:	Three 7.62mm (0.3in) DT machine-guns (one co-axial, one in hull, one in rear of turret)
Combat Weight:	47.5 tons
Length:	6.25m (20ft 6in)
Width:	3.25m (10ft 9in)
Height:	2.75m (9ft)
Road Speed:	35km/h (22mph)
Road Range:	250km (155mls)
Crew:	Five

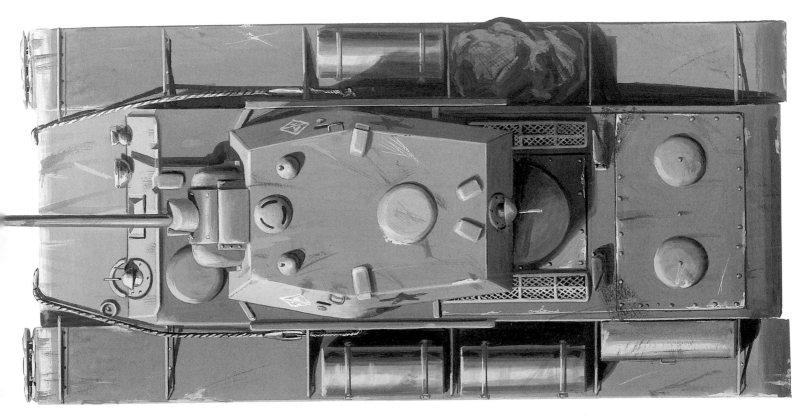

SU-76 Light Self-propelled Gun

Second only in numbers to the T-34 among Soviet armoured vehicles, 12,661 of the SU-76 'Light Mechanised Gun' were built up to 1945. The original version produced from December 1942 had separate engines for each track and the main gun exactly on the centreline; on later models it was shifted to the left. This allowed the engine compartment to be placed on the right, with one engine behind the other and a single gearbox, a much less complex arrangement. The obsolete T-70 tank on which the SU-76 was based had this arrangement and this story proves the old adage, 'if it ain't broke, don't fix it!' The main production version was the SU-76M which was produced from May 1943, was lightly armoured with only 35mm (1.3in) of armour on the upper hull and no overhead covering stronger than a tarpaulin for the gun crew. The gun was able to traverse 32 degrees within its mount. The ZIS-3 'divisional gun' had a rate of fire of 12 rounds per minute and was the obvious choice for a Samokhodnaya Ustanovka (self-propelled mounting) having proved itself as an excellent artillery piece and anti-tank gun. By the time the SU-76 was available in numbers, however, this gun had passed its prime and could easily be outranged by most German anti-tank guns. The lack of protection or creature comforts (the driver sat directly next to the throbbing engines) led to the nickname Sukami (bitch) for these early SU vehicles. With newer assault guns available, the SU-76s were relegated to indirect fire-support roles before long, and many were converted to anti-aircraft mounts. The Germans were astonished in early 1944 to find a version called the SU-76i which had the same superstructure and armament as the M, but which was mounted on captured Panzer III chassis. Twice as heavy, there were more than 200 so converted and they were used in the same fashion as the 'Russian' SUs. Despite, or perhaps because of, their unpopularity with crews, SU-76Ms were distributed to many Soviet 'client states' after the war and could be found in some armies up to the 1980s.

Specification

Country of Origin:	Soviet Union
Main Armament:	One 76.2mm (3in) ZIS-3 cannon
Secondary Armament:	One 7.62mm (0.3in) DT machine-gun
Combat Weight:	11.2 tons
Length:	6.37m (16ft 3in)
Width:	2.74m (9ft)
Height:	2.20m (6ft 9in)
Road Speed:	45km/h (28mph)
Road Range:	320km (198mls)
Crew:	Four

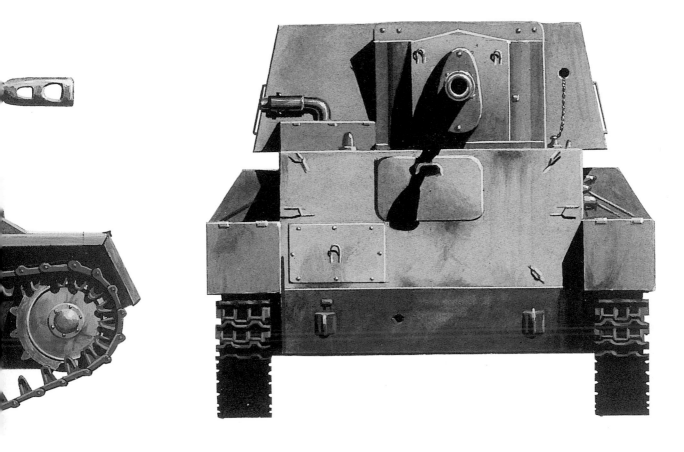

KV-85 Heavy Tank

The KV-85's designation hints at its origin, as a development of the KV-1 heavy tank with an 85mm (3.4in) gun. The last KV-1 model, the KV-1S, which retained a 76.2mm (3in) gun, had many improvements over its predecessors and most of these were incorporated in the KV-85. Going against all trends of tank development, the KV-1S and KV-85 had less armour than earlier models (down from 130mm to 60mm (5.1in to 2.3in) on the hull sides for example) but this gave it 25 per cent greater speed and better mobility. The same V-12 447kW (600hp) diesel engine now gave a 9.7kW (13.1hp) per ton power-to-weight ratio. An entirely new cast steel turret of the type designed for the IS-1 was fitted and this featured a commander's cupola for the first time on a KV-series tank. The rear-facing machine-gun was eliminated and the crew was reduced from five to four, comprising a commander, a driver, a loader/mechanic and a gunner. Production began in the autumn of 1943 and the 27th Independent Guard Tank Penetration Regiment took the KV-85 into action in early December where it suffered heavy losses. The KV-85 was designed to counter the increasing number of Tigers appearing on the battlefield, but while the two were roughly equally matched, the Tiger had the bigger gun, the thicker armour, and usually, the greater numbers, so won most encounters on the open steppes of Russia and the Ukraine. Seen as an interim design of which only 130 were produced, all in 1943, the KV-85 was the last tank in the KV series, although it was the basis for several self-propelled assault guns.

Specification
Country of Origin: Soviet Union
Main Armament: One 85mm (3.4in) 1943 (D-5T) cannon
Secondary Armament: Two 7.6mm (0.3in) DT machine-guns (one co-axial, one in hull)
Combat Weight: 46 tons
Length: 8.6m (28ft 2in)
Width: 3.25m (10ft 9in)
Height: 2.8m (9ft 2in)
Road Speed: 42km/h (26mph)
Road Range: 330km (205mls)
Crew: Four

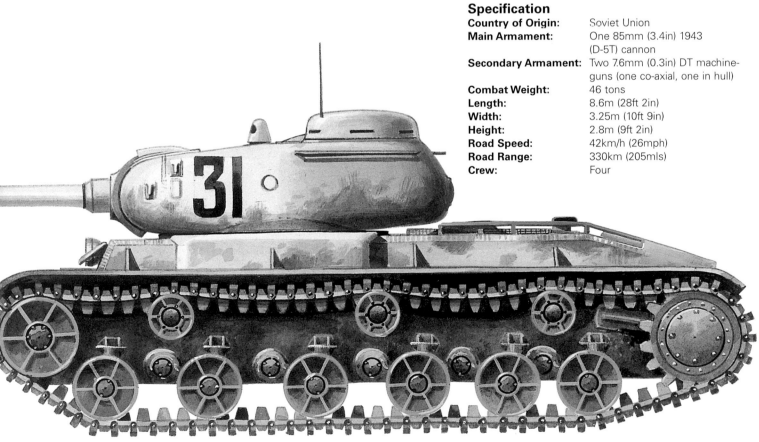

IS-2 (Iosef Stalin) Heavy Tank

The IS-2 (Iosef Stalin) combined the best features of
the KV-series tanks with the firepower of a naval
destroyer. It was essentially the same as the IS (Iosef
Stalin) 1, derived from the KV-85, which had been
produced from December 1943, and shared its
improved gearbox and better distribution of armour.
The main difference was its huge 122mm (4.8in) D-25T
gun, which fired a projectile with over three times the
kinetic energy of the 76.2mm (3in) round, the heaviest
in service in 1941. Even if it failed to penetrate the armour of a German Panther or Tiger,
the explosive charge in the 25kg (55lb) shell was often enough to blow the turret off its
mount. One disadvantage of this weapon, which itself weighed nearly two tons, was that
the shell and cartridge were separate and had to be combined before firing. This restricted
the rate of fire to three rounds per minute at best. Both 100mm (3.9in) and 122mm (4.8in)
guns had been proposed for the IS-2, the former proving superior in trials, but it was easier
to mass-produce the 122 and its ammunition and it was officially chosen in late December
1943. The first IS-2s saw combat in February 1944. Of the weapons encountered at that
time, only the 88mm (3.5in) gun of the Tiger I had any chance of penetrating the 160mm
(6.2in) frontal armour at long range. The IS-2 could defeat a Panther at 1500m (1640yds),
but the Panther had to get as close as 400m (440yds) to have any chance of victory. Many
IS-1s were rebuilt with the new gun and both types led the spearhead of the Soviet army
to Berlin. Approximately 2500 IS-2s were built before the IS-3 replaced it in production in
early 1945. Some were rebuilt as armoured recovery vehicles, being the only machine able
to recover damaged IS-2s on the battlefield.

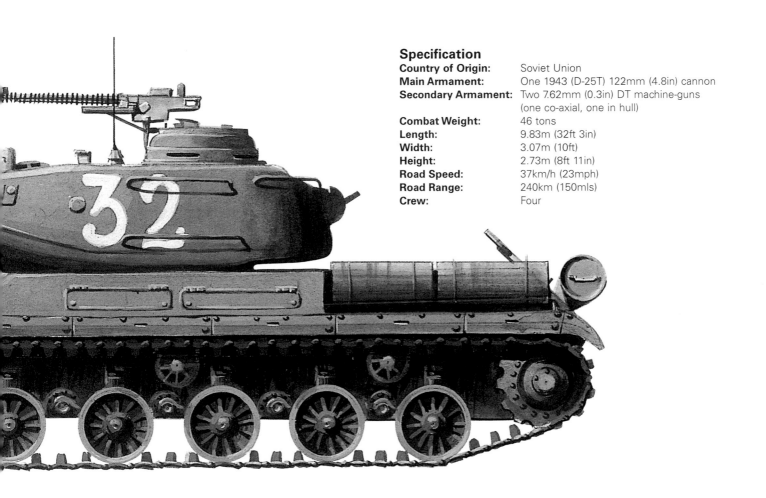

Specification

Country of Origin:	Soviet Union
Main Armament:	One 1943 (D-25T) 122mm (4.8in) cannon
Secondary Armament:	Two 7.62mm (0.3in) DT machine-guns (one co-axial, one in hull)
Combat Weight:	46 tons
Length:	9.83m (32ft 3in)
Width:	3.07m (10ft)
Height:	2.73m (8ft 11in)
Road Speed:	37km/h (23mph)
Road Range:	240km (150mls)
Crew:	Four

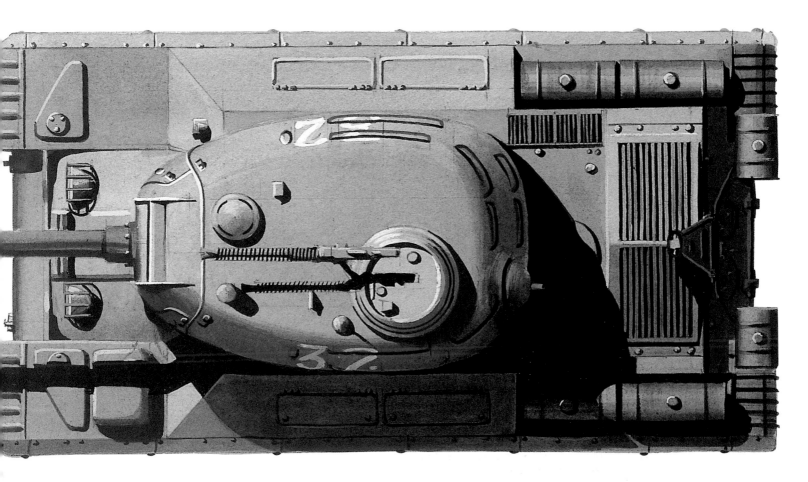

SU-152 Heavy Assault Gun

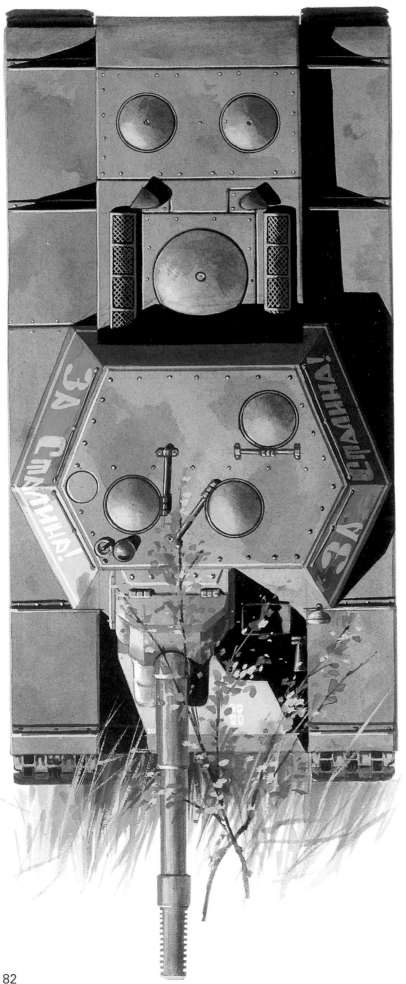

German success with heavy assault guns used in the anti-tank role caused Soviet tank designers to evaluate this type of vehicle in 1942. The team behind the KV-1 heavy tank adapted several examples with new casemate hulls and 76.2mm (3in) guns. One of these, designated the KV-7, had two guns mounted in parallel, which looked impressive but had little effect on hitting power. The new hull design was adopted, however, for the carriage of a massive 152mm (5.9in) 'corps howitzer-cannon'. This gun was a field artillery piece designed for both long range artillery support (indirect fire) and direct assault on fortifications. When mounted in the new vehicle, which was accepted as the SU-152 in early 1943, it could fire a 52kg (114lb) high-explosive shell over 5km (3.1mls) and a lighter anti-tank shell the same distance with less elevation. One of the best features of the SU-152 was its low profile, a characteristic not found in earlier Soviet self-propelled guns. A penalty of this compact arrangement was the cramped interior, and as few as 20 rounds and their cartridges could be carried internally. This meant that the 152s needed an entourage of ammunition carriers or to stay close to field howitzer positions if they were to have any combat persistence. Like other Soviet AFVs, the SU-152 was often the carriage for 'tank descent squads', platoons of infantry hitching a lift into battle. These proved especially useful in the case of the assault guns that were usually only fitted with a machine-gun for anti-aircraft defence and made use of the soldiers for self-protection. The SU-152's debut was at Kursk in July 1943, where they led the counterattack alongside the medium tanks and were an important part of the Soviet victory. The SU-152 and its successor, based on the Josef Stalin 2 and designated ISU-152, blasted their way through fortifications and armour all the way to Berlin with the largest gun mounted on a production AFV during World War II.

Specification

Country of Origin: Soviet Union
Main Armament: One 152mm (5.9in) 1937 (ML-20S) howitzer-cannon
Secondary Armament: One 7.62mm (0.3in) DT machine-gun
Combat Weight: 45.5 tons
Length: 8.95m (29ft 4in); hull length: 6.75m (22ft 1in)
Width: 3.25m (10ft 9in)
Height: 2.45m (8ft 1in)
Road Speed: 43km/h (27mph)
Road Range: 320km (198mls)
Crew: Five

Mk III, Valentine I Infantry Tank

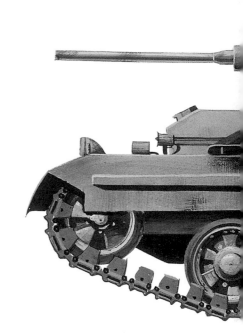

Named Valentine because Vickers submitted its design to the War Office just before the deadline of 14 February 1938, the Infantry Tank Mk III was a development of the A10 Heavy Cruiser, already produced by the firm. With war looming in Europe, a substantial order was made in July 1939 and by late 1940 the first examples were in service. The 8th Army was equipped with many Valentines by mid-1941 and the type played a major role in fighting in the Western Desert. The Valentine suffered from the deficiencies of most British tanks of the period, namely poor firepower and armour protection compared to its opponents, but was one of the more reliable tanks as most of the mechanical problems of the A10 had been designed out. One of the failings of the early models was the small two-man turret that forced the gunner to take his eye off the target to reload the gun himself. The Valentine III introduced a larger three-man turret with the commander's position moved towards the rear and provision for a loader, increasing the crew to four. Some Valentine IIIs were equipped with DD (Duplex Drive) equipment and side-skirts so that they could 'swim' ashore from landing craft. By the time of the Normandy landings the Valentine DDs were replaced by Sherman DDs, but they helped develop operational methods and train crews of the 79th Armoured Division. The Valentine's importance was more in its numbers (8275 produced) than in its quality. The Montreal Locomotive Works produced 1420 Valentines and the great majority of these were supplied to the Soviet army. Other Valentines were supplied to the Australian and New Zealand armies where they were mainly used for training.

Specification

Country of Origin:	Great Britain
Main Armament:	One 2pdr (40mm/1.6in) cannon
Secondary Armament:	One co-axial 7.92mm (0.3in) Besa machine-gun, one turret-mounted Bren machine-gun
Combat Weight:	17.7 tons
Length:	5.41m (17ft 9in)
Width:	2.63m (8ft 7.5in)
Height:	2.27m (7ft 5.5in)
Road Speed:	24km/h (15mph)
Road Range:	145km (90mls)
Crew:	Three

Mk VI, Crusader I Cruiser Tank

One of the most distinctive British tanks of the war, the Crusader was also one of the least effective, suffering from a rushed development and an outmoded design concept. It began as a private venture by the Nuffield organisation to create a 'heavy cruiser' development of their earlier Cruiser IV. As such the Crusader, which was ordered in July 1939, had the same engine and turret as the earlier tank, although it was lengthened and had greater armour protection all round. With the worsening war situation, orders for 200 were followed by another 200 and then a further 662 in quick succession. By the end of production in

1943, 5300 had been built. Abbreviated trials of the pilot model in 1939 had shown up poor ventilation and engine cooling and a troublesome gearbox. These problems became more apparent when the Crusader first saw combat in the Western Desert in June 1941. Solutions to some of these problems were found: they had to be, as the Crusader was numerically one of the most important tanks in the theatre. The poorly ventilated front turret was removed from many Mk Is and this allowed the crew to be reduced to a more comfortable four, although the gunner's space was usually filled with more ammunition. The Mk III, available by

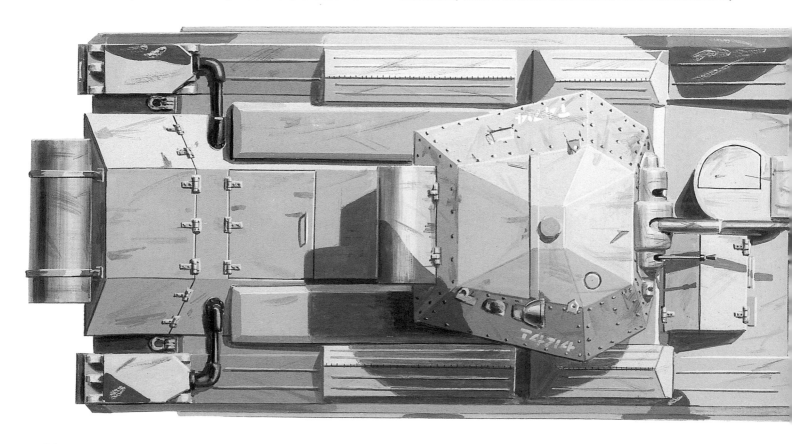

mid-1942, went some way towards correcting the Crusader's main weakness – its lack of firepower – by introducing the 6pdr gun in place of the original 2pdr and was the main variant in service by the time of the Battle of El Alamein. Nonetheless, the guns of the German panzers at the time, not to speak of the anti-tank guns of various calibres, could usually pick off Crusaders at long range, despite their relative speed and small size. By May 1943, the last were retired from front line service, although special purpose versions (AA tanks, recovery vehicles and gun tractors) were in use after D-Day in Northwest Europe.

Specification

Country of Origin:	Great Britain
Main Armament:	One 2pdr (40mm/1.6in) OQF cannon
Secondary Armament:	Two 7.92mm (0.3in) Besa machine-guns (one co-axial, one in front turret)
Combat Weight:	19 tons
Length:	5.99m (19ft 8in)
Width:	2.64m (8ft 8in)
Height:	2.23m (7ft 4in)
Road Speed:	43km/h (27mph)
Road Range:	160km (100mls)
Crew:	Five

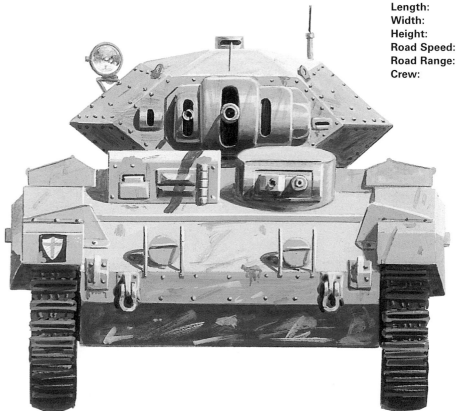

Mk IVA Cruiser Tank

Also known by the ordnance designation A13 Mk II, the Cruiser Mk IV was an up-armoured version of the Cruiser Mk III (A13). In early 1939 it had been decided that all Cruiser-type tanks should have a minimum armour thickness of 30mm (1.1in). The additional armour on the nose, glacis and turret added 544kg (1200lbs) to the weight, but did not greatly affect the performance or handling due to the high power-to-weight ratio provided by the Nuffield Liberty V-12 engine. The v-section armour on the turret sides was the main distinguishing feature compared to the Cruiser III and gave a 'spaced armour' effect, killing the energy of a shell before it struck the turret proper. The Mk IVA differed mainly in having a Besa machine-gun, which became the standard secondary weapon on British tanks, in place of the Vickers gun of the Mk IV. The Mk IVCS was a version with a 93.9mm (3.7in) mortar in place of the 2pdr OQF (Ordnance Quick-Firing) cannon. The 1st Armoured Division used the Cruiser Mk IV in France in 1940 and the 7th Armoured Division used it in the Western Desert where its high speed was valued. After 1941, they were mainly used for training in the UK. Total production of 655 examples was split between prime contractor Nuffield, and LMS, Leyland and English Electric.

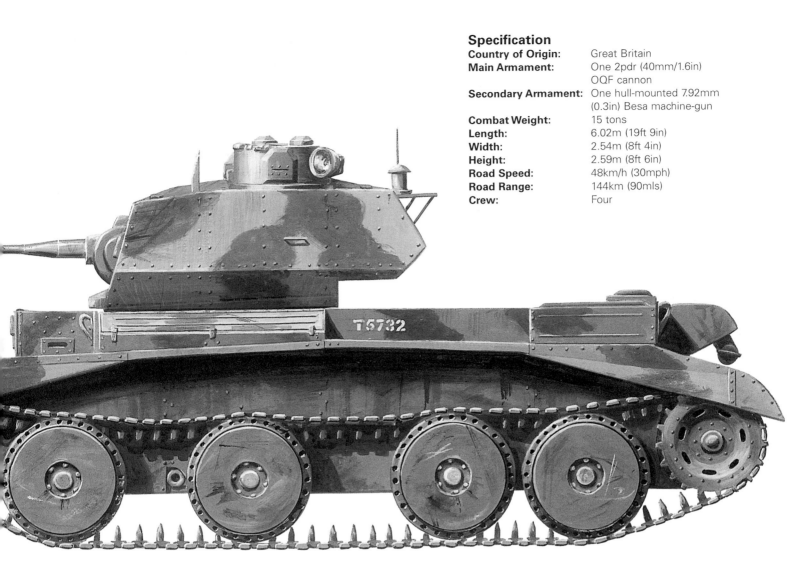

Specification

Country of Origin:	Great Britain
Main Armament:	One 2pdr (40mm/1.6in) OQF cannon
Secondary Armament:	One hull-mounted 7.92mm (0.3in) Besa machine-gun
Combat Weight:	15 tons
Length:	6.02m (19ft 9in)
Width:	2.54m (8ft 4in)
Height:	2.59m (8ft 6in)
Road Speed:	48km/h (30mph)
Road Range:	144km (90mls)
Crew:	Four

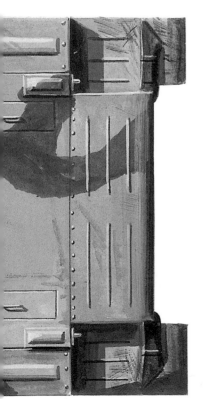

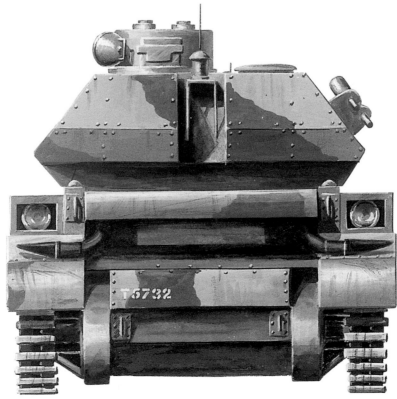

Mk IV Churchill IV Infantry Tank

The Churchill was the last of the so-called 'infantry' tanks built by the British. The design reflected the World War I practice in that it had a long hull and tracks for trench crossing and travelled at a speed across shell-churned ground that soldiers could match. The specification was drawn up at the outbreak of war in September 1939 and a pilot model had been produced within five months. This featured two 2pdr (40mm/1.6in) guns and two hull-mounted machine guns and a crew of seven. Because of its excessive weight and troublesome gearbox, the design was scaled down, the armament was halved and many detail changes were made. By June 1941 the first of an order for 500 Churchill Is were rolled out. These and the next batch of the same size needed extensive modification before they could be issued to the troops. The combat debut came on the abortive Dieppe raid in May 1942 when many Churchills failed to reach the beach, let alone support the infantry any distance inland. The Churchill IV, first produced in mid-1942, corrected many of the faults of the earlier models, which tended to be with minor components, although the innovative transmission system had often been troublesome. The Churchill III and IV were fitted with a 6pdr (57mm/2.2in) gun, usually the OQF (Ordnance Quick Firing) Mk V with its distinctive muzzle-end counterweight on the latter variant. This was a 'single-purpose' gun like the 2pdr; able to fire armour piercing (AP) but not high explosive (HE) rounds. Until the development of later specialised models, Churchills had to rely on other units such as field artillery or naval ships for close support. At Dieppe this proved a distinct disadvantage as the tanks faced mainly fixed or un-armoured targets where HE would have been more useful. Despite its outmoded design, the Churchill proved a well-armoured and useful tank in Tunisia and in the Normandy campaign. Designed to fit the loading-gauge of British railways, the Churchill was too narrow to accept the larger turret ring needed to mount a bigger gun. Many uses were found for Churchills other than as main battle tanks, particularly as recovery and engineering vehicles and for specialised obstacle clearance tasks.

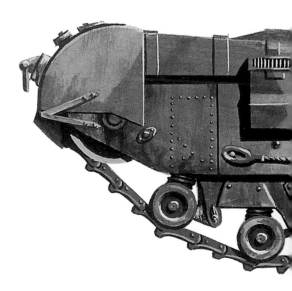

Specification

Country of Origin:	Great Britain
Main Armament:	One 6pdr (57mm/2.2in) OQF Mk V cannon
Secondary Armament:	Two co-axial 7.92mm (0.3in) Besa machine-guns
Combat Weight:	39.6 tons
Length:	7.44m (24ft 5in)
Width:	2.74m (9ft)
Height:	3.25m (10ft 8in)
Road Speed:	24km/h (15mph)
Road Range:	144km (90mls)
Crew:	Five

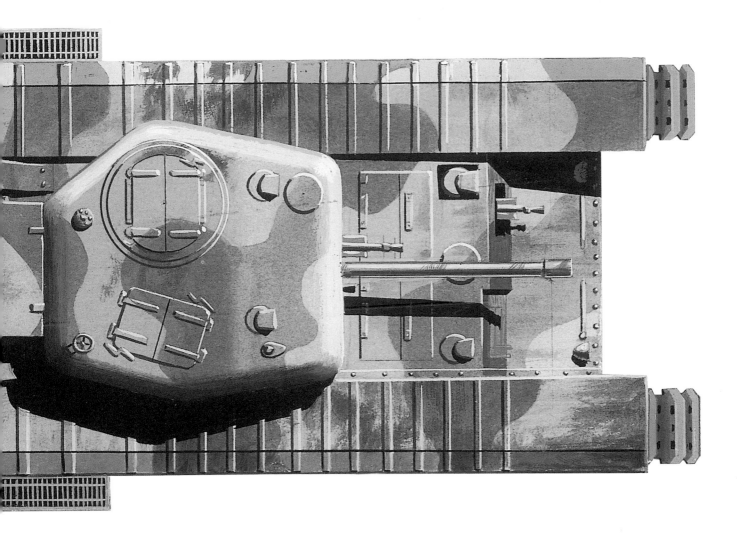

AEC Mk III Armoured Car

Designed (and built) by a bus manufacturer without any official requirement, the AEC armoured cars proved to be the equal of many tanks of their day and served with distinction in North Africa and Europe. In 1941, the AEC (Associated Engineering Company) of Southall, West London built an armoured car based on information they had gleaned on fighting in North Africa. This Mk I car was virtually a wheeled tank, with heavy armour, a powerful engine and a 2pdr (40mm/1.6in) gun, equivalent to that used by most tanks in the desert. In fact its turret came from the Valentine cruiser tank. The War Office accepted this private-venture design and an order was placed for over 120 AEC Mk Is. Armament was increased on subsequent models in parallel with developments in tank guns. The AEC Mk II was given a three-man electrically-traversed turret and a 6pdr (57mm/2.2in) gun, but the Mk III had a 75mm (2.9in) M3 cannon as used on most US medium tanks. This was an exceptionally large gun for an Allied armoured car, and the high speed of the AEC made it valuable as a hit-and-run weapon, especially in North Africa. The AECs had selectable two- or four-wheel drive and steering with front-wheel drive used only for road travel. One of the few faults of these cars was its high profile and angular appearance, which made it hard to conceal in the observation role. As illustrated here, natural foliage was often used to break up the outline. In general, the AEC IIIs provided fire support when needed for the lighter Daimlers and Humbers that made up the bulk of the armoured car companies. After the North African campaign, the AECs saw most service in Italy and a number were supplied to Yugoslav partisans. Others served with the heavy troops of the armoured car companies in the Northwest Europe campaign. After the war, some were supplied to Belgium for its reconnaissance regiments. Total production of the three models was 629 vehicles.

Specification

Country of Origin:	Great Britain
Main Armament:	One 75mm (2.9in) M3 cannon
Secondary Armament:	One co-axial 7.92mm (0.3in) Besa machine-gun
Combat Weight:	12.7 tons
Length:	5.61m (18ft 5in)
Width:	2.70m (8ft 11in)
Height:	2.69m (8ft 10in)
Road Speed:	58km/h (36mph)
Road Range:	400km (250mls)
Crew:	Four

Mk VIII, Cromwell VI Cruiser Tank

Built to a 1941 General Staff Requirement for a 'heavy cruiser', the Cromwell design took account of experience with the Crusader showing that speed was no substitute for armour and firepower. Fifty per cent heavier than the Crusader due to its increased armour (up to 76mm/2.9in), the Cromwell compensated for its extra weight by having the powerful Rolls-Royce Meteor engine, which was a version of the famous Merlin aero engine used in the Spitfire, Lancaster and many other aircraft. The V-12 Meteor was the first truly reliable engine fitted to a British tank and made the Cromwell the fastest British tank of the war years: in fact it was a bit too fast for its suspension, which tended to wear too quickly, and later versions were de-tuned to reduce top speed in favour of overall maintainability. Production started at Leyland Motors from January 1943 onwards and the initial Cromwell I was soon followed in production with the improved Cromwell II and III, all with the tried and tested 6pdr (57mm/2.2in) gun. The Cromwell Mk IV which entered service in October 1943 introduced a 75mm (2.9in) gun and this was used on all versions up to the Mk VIII which sported a 95mm (3.7in) close-support howitzer. By the time of the Normandy landings, the British tank regiments were mainly equipping with the American Sherman, but the Cromwell still saw considerable action with the 7th Armoured Division in Northwest Europe. With its well-tried Christie suspension, powerful engine, and good protection, the Cromwell gave British tank crews the opportunity to be at par with their German opponents. Variants of the basic design included the Cromwell ARV (Armoured Recovery Vehicle) and the Cromwell OP mobile artillery observation post. The Cromwell served as a stepping stone to the superior Comet which was to see limited action before the war's end and considerable service post-war.

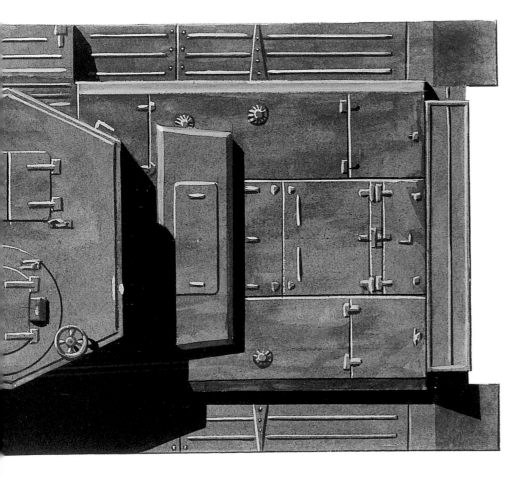

Specification

Country of Origin: Great Britain
Main Armament: One 75mm (2.9in) QQF cannon
Secondary Armament: Two 7.92mm (0.3in) Besa machine-guns (one hull-mounted, one co-axial)
Combat Weight: 28 tons
Length: 6.42m (21ft 9in)
Width: 3.48m (10ft)
Height: 2.51m (8ft 3in)
Road Speed: 61km/h (38mph)
Road Range: 278km (173mls)
Crew: Five

Mk Churchill VII Crocodile Infantry/Flame-thrower Tank

The Churchill Crocodile was one of the extremely specialised vehicles developed by the British in preparation for Operation Overlord, the planned invasion of Northwest Europe. Knowing that the entire Atlantic coast of France was fortified with every type of anti-tank obstacle, bunker and gun emplacement, British High Command formed a special new unit, the 79th Armoured Division, to develop weapons and tactics for crossing the vital few yards of beach at the beginning of the invasion. The 79th was led by Major-General Percy Hobart, and the numerous specialised tanks converted for his division were collectively known as 'Hobart's Funnies' or simply 'Funnies'. Amongst the Funnies were mine flail and mine roller tanks, bridge-layers, 'swimming' tanks, assault mortars and flame-throwers. One of these latter vehicles was a conversion of the Churchill VII medium tank which towed a

trailer loaded with fuel with a motion suggestive of a crocodile crawling out of the water. Although superficially similar to earlier models, the Churchill VII was of completely new construction with no hull frame, instead being constructed from frameless armour plate which was joined to form a rigid structure. A new cast/welded heavy turret with a commander's cupola was fitted, as was an improved gearbox, new escape doors and other detail refinements. The main difference from earlier marks was the 75mm (2.9in) MV (Medium Velocity) cannon, which replaced the outdated 57mm (2.2in) of earlier versions. The Crocodile conversion, of which 800 were made by the end of the war, involved replacing the hull machine-gun with a projector capable of emitting a jet of flame 73–100m (80–120yds) long. This was fed under nitrogen pressure by a pipe from the 6.5-ton armoured

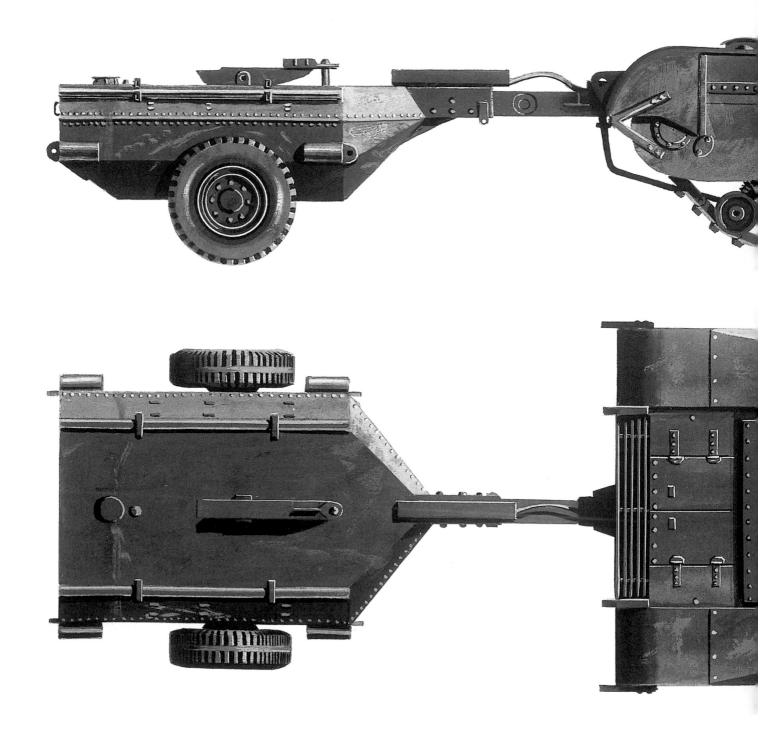

trailer. Unlike some other flame-thrower tanks, the Crocodile could use its main gun at the same time as its projector and retained its co-axial machine-gun. The trailer, which could be jettisoned when empty or hit, had enough fuel for 80 one-second bursts of fire. On D-Day, the Crocodiles were used against bunkers and machine-gun positions on the beach, and throughout the rest of the war as flame-throwers or conventional tanks as the situation dictated.

Specification

Country of Origin:	Great Britain
Main Armament:	One flame projector, one 75mm (2.9in) MV cannon
Secondary Armament:	One co-axial 7.92mm (0.3in) Besa machine-gun
Combat Weight:	40.6 tons, plus trailer 6.5 tons
Length:	7.44m (24ft 5in)
Width:	2.74m (9ft)
Height:	3.45m (11ft 4in)
Road Speed:	20km/h (12.5mph)
Road Range:	144km (90mls)
Crew:	Five

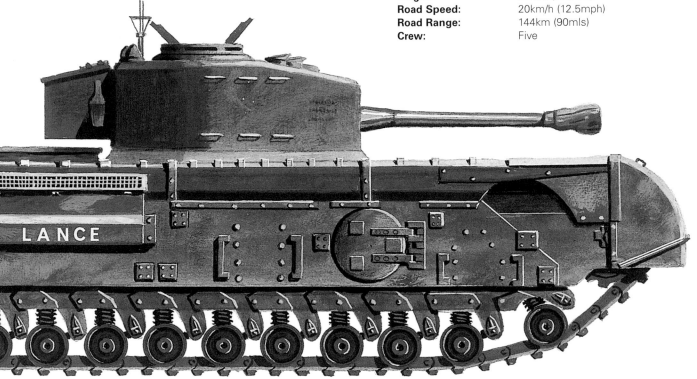

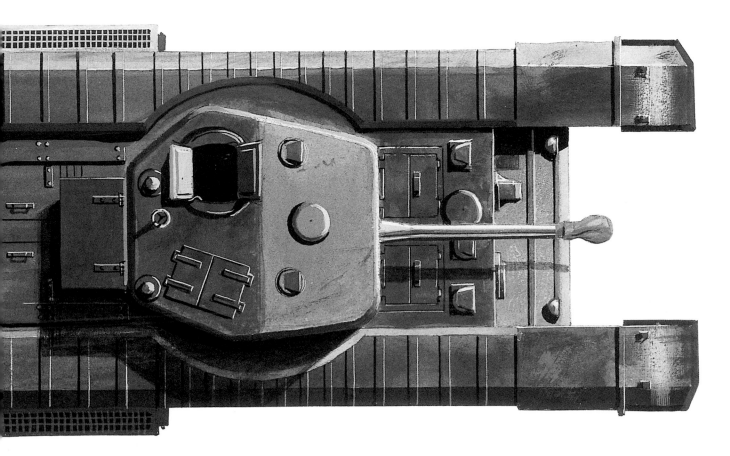

Churchill AVRE Assault Tank

The raid on the French port of Dieppe in May 1942 showed up the need for dedicated specialised tanks to clear beach obstacles and defences for the fighting vehicles in the first wave of an invasion. Many tanks (mostly Churchills) were caught on anti-tank obstacles and destroyed by crossfire from fixed bunkers pre-sighted on the beach. Engineers could blow up some of the beach obstacles if they could reach them alive, and ditches and streams could be crossed with temporary bridges that could be laid by tanks. From these requirements came the Churchill AVRE (Armoured Vehicle, Royal Engineers) which came in many forms but basically was an early form of armoured personnel carrier (APC) or infantry fighting vehicle (IFV) with a large mortar and some type of obstacle clearing equipment. The roomy hull and large escape doors of the Churchill allowed a party of combat engineers to be carried and deposited on the beach or battlefield to clear obstructions. The AVRE's main weapon, a 290mm (11.4in) 'recoiling spigot mortar' or 'petard mortar' could fire a 18.1kg (40lb) demolition bomb a distance of about 73m (80yds) at enemy bunkers or strongpoints. The 'flying dustbins' were not very accurate but their blast would usually disable a gun emplacement and stun its occupants long enough for other tanks or infantry to finish the job. Each AVRE had an alternative purpose, in this case to lay a log carpet for other tanks to follow across marshy or boggy ground. A similar function was carried out by AVREs with large brushwood bundles or 'fascines' which would be dropped into ditches or narrow water obstacles, compressing to fill the gap as the AVRE and following tanks drove over them. Pushed over the far side of wall defences, they could be used to reduce the drop for tanks climbing over the top. In preparation for the Normandy landings, 180 conversions of standard Churchill IVs were made to AVRE tanks for the 79th Armoured Division. They proved their worth on the 6th of June 1944 and afterwards when they saved many Allied lives. New versions were built after the war and the last were retired as late as 1965.

Specification

Country of Origin:	Great Britain
Main Armament:	One 290mm (11.4in) mortar
Secondary Armament:	Two co-axial 7.92mm (0.3in) Besa machine-guns
Combat Weight:	39.6 tons
Length:	7.44m (24ft 5in)
Width:	2.74m (9ft)
Height:	4.24m (10ft 8in) to top of frame
Road Speed:	24km/h (15mph)
Road Range:	144km (90mls)
Crew:	Five plus engineer party

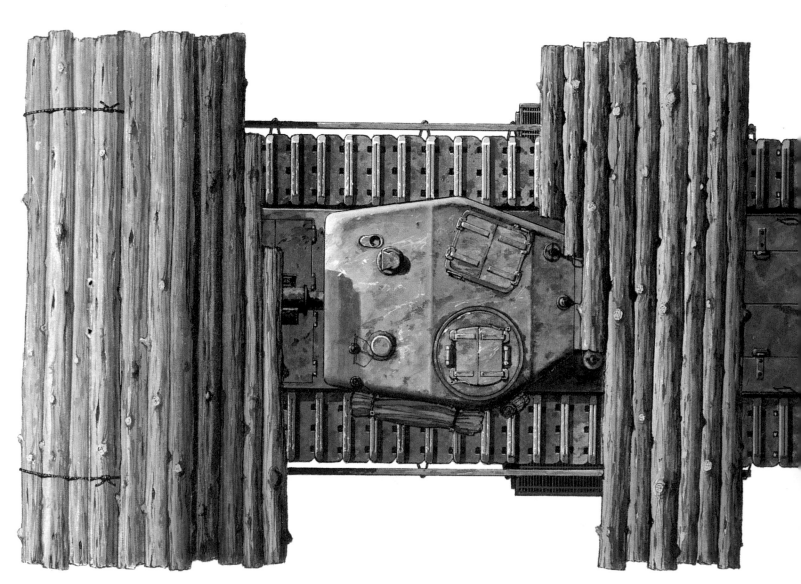

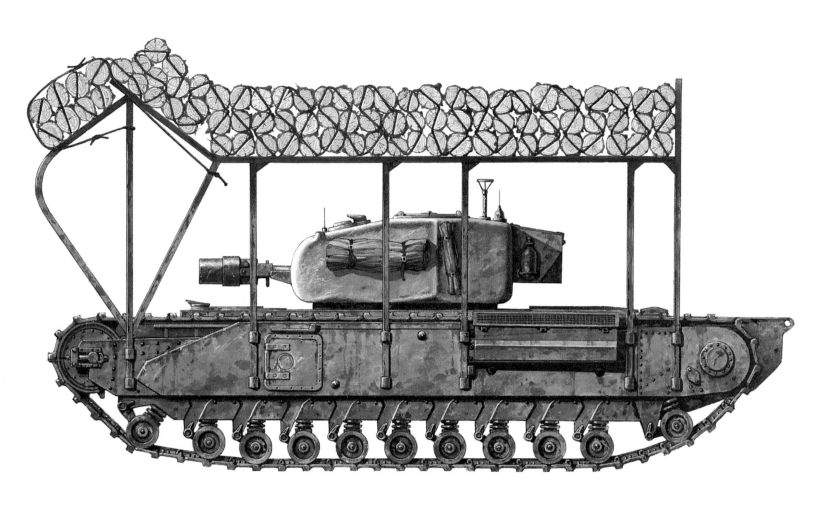

Sherman Crab II (Sherman V) Mine-clearing Tank

Specification

Country of Origin:	USA/Great Britain
Main Armament:	One 75mm (2.9in) M3 cannon
Secondary Armament:	One co-axial 7.6mm (0.3in) machine-gun
Combat Weight:	31.1 tons without flail
Length:	8.73m (28ft 7in) including flail rig
Width:	3.25m (8ft 7in) including flail rig
Height:	2.74m (9ft)
Road Speed:	40km/h (25mph) without flail
Road Range:	240km (150mls) without flail
Crew:	Five

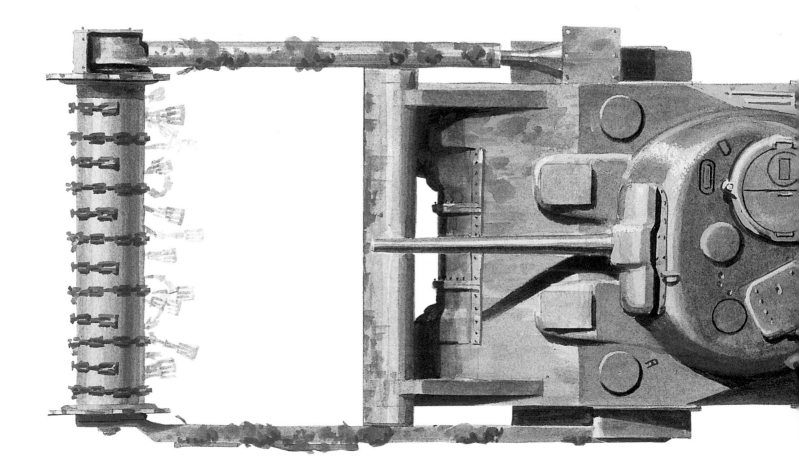

The US-built M4 Sherman is the best-known tank of the World War II era. It was the principal tank of the Western Allies from 1942 and was built in greater numbers than any tank outside the Soviet Union. The total of 48,000 Shermans and variants exceeds the total of all German tanks, tank destroyers and assault guns produced during the war years. The Sherman spawned an astonishing number of variants; assault guns, recovery vehicles, rocket launchers and flame-throwers, gun carriages and bridgelayers. Some of the most unusual were created by the British for the specialised business of crossing the few yards of heavily defended beach of the Normandy coast. One of these was the Sherman Crab which was equipped with a mine 'flail' at the end of long hydraulic arms. This device was powered by a shaft drive from the tank's own engine and was basically a rotating drum to which was fixed 43 heavy chains that would thrash the beach and detonate any mines buried beneath the surface. The danger to tanks was from mines exploding directly beneath the tracks, so the shrapnel from nearby explosions was not a great threat to the Crab tank itself. These vehicles were almost exclusively developed for use by the British 79th Armoured Division, and their use was one of the reasons for relatively low casualties and good progress made by the British and Canadians on D-Day itself compared to US forces. Later in 1944, the Crab II was introduced for dealing with inland minefields on rough terrain where mines could be missed. The Crab II had a contour-following device, which was basically an extra weight on the left-hand arm that forced the flail rig into dips in the ground. At the rear of the Crab tanks were station-keeping devices and lane-marker dispensers so that the correct parts of the beach were swept and the clear lanes were kept to by the other vehicles. The USA adopted a few as the T3 Mine Exploder, but mainly used giant rollers pushed by M4s to clear mines.

M4A4 Sherman VC Firefly Medium Tank

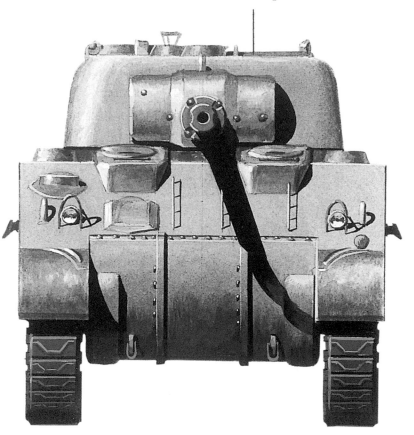

The American M4 medium tank proved to be not only the most important US tank used during the war, but also the best and most numerous tank in British service. As was the practice of the time, the British named the M4 after an American general (in this case Civil War general William Tecumseh Sherman, famous for the quotation 'War is Hell') and the Americans adopted the name.

M3 Sherman Mk Is were first used at El Alamein in October 1942 and the British introduced most of the US versions as they became available, namely the Sherman II (M4A1), Sherman III (M4A2), Sherman IV (M4A3) and Sherman V (M4A4). Suffix

letters denoted the main armament fitted, C indicating the 17pdr Ordnance Quick-Firing gun. Existing British tanks proved incapable of taking a turret large enough to mount the 17pdr anti-tank gun which, like its predecessors, had been designed for both tank and anti-tank use. In the Sherman, the gun could only just be fitted by mounting it on its side and adapting it for left-hand loading, but the conversion proved possible without enlarging the turret ring. The first Sherman VC pilot model was ready in November 1943 and priority production was ordered in February 1944. This was too late for large numbers to be available for the D-Day landings, so the Firefly, as it was dubbed, was issued on the basis of one per each troop of regular 75mm (2.9in) Shermans. The Sherman Firefly was the only British tank able to meet the German Panther and Tiger I on roughly equal terms. Its gun was more accurate and longer-ranged than previous Allied tank guns and was able to penetrate 120mm (4.7in) armour at 500m (1500ft). Tactics against the German heavy tanks became a business of distracting the enemy with the three 'regular' Shermans while the Firefly got into a good firing position from the side. In general, two Shermans were lost for every Panther or Tiger destroyed in combat, but whereas German industry could not make up their losses by mid-1944, the US and British production lines were delivering a seemingly endless supply of Shermans and other tanks. By early 1945, most British tank troops in Europe were fully equipped with Fireflies.

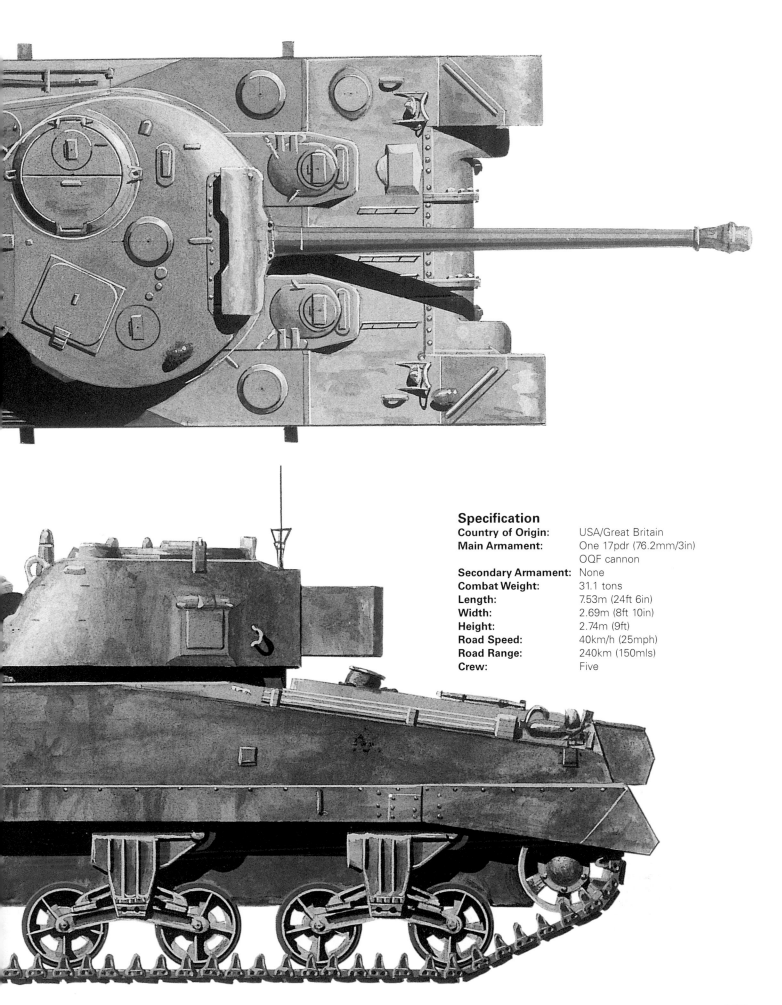

Specification

Country of Origin:	USA/Great Britain
Main Armament:	One 17pdr (76.2mm/3in) OQF cannon
Secondary Armament:	None
Combat Weight:	31.1 tons
Length:	7.53m (24ft 6in)
Width:	2.69m (8ft 10in)
Height:	2.74m (9ft)
Road Speed:	40km/h (25mph)
Road Range:	240km (150mls)
Crew:	Five

L3-35/Lf Light Flame-thrower Tank

Italy specialised in light tanks with only a few designs in the medium category. Those light tanks designed pre-war were close relatives of a British Carden-Lloyd tankette design, examples of which had been purchased in 1929. The Italians named their versions Carro Veloce (fast tank) and the most important, the CV 33, was designed in 1933 and entered service two years later. Over 1300 were produced by Fiat-Ansaldo in the first order alone, some for export to countries including Afghanistan, Albania, Bolivia, Brazil, China and Nationalist Spain. These extremely simple little vehicles had no turret as such; a rear-mounted petrol engine and front-wheel drive, and one or two light machine-guns as the main armament. The hull was of riveted and bolted construction as were the majority of Italian tanks, the armour plate being only 5–15mm (0.2–0.6in) thick. One interesting feature of the CV 33 was its air-portability. The tank (or more correctly, tankette) could be slung under a transport aircraft, an idea later taken up by the Americans for airborne forces use. Twin machine-gun versions were unofficially known as CV 35s, and the final production version was the CV L38, some of which rebuilt with a 20mm (0.7in) cannon. The ability of the CV tanks to tow an ammunition trailer (having evolved from what was essentially a light weapons tractor) was used in a flame-thrower version. The jellied petroleum (napalm) was kept in a 500kg (half-ton) trailer and piped forward to the flame projector, which was mounted in the centre of the superstructure face. This idea was used later by the British in the Normandy landings. This version was called the L35/Lf at first and, after 1940, the L3-35Lf with Lf standing for 'lanciafiamme' or flame-thrower. The type was called a 'Carro d'assalto lancia-fiamme' or flame-thrower assault tank. On later versions the flame equipment (fuel tank etc.) was mounted on the back of the tank, as seen here. With the Italian armistice in 1943, the Germans took over the survivors of the 2000 CV tanks built and issued them mostly to police and labour camp units.

Specification

Country of Origin:	Italy
Main Armament:	One flame projector
Secondary Armament:	None
Combat weight:	3.1 tons
Length:	3.2m (10ft 5in)
Width:	1.42m (4ft 8in)
Height:	1.30m (4ft 3in)
Road Speed:	42km/h (26mph)
Crew:	Two

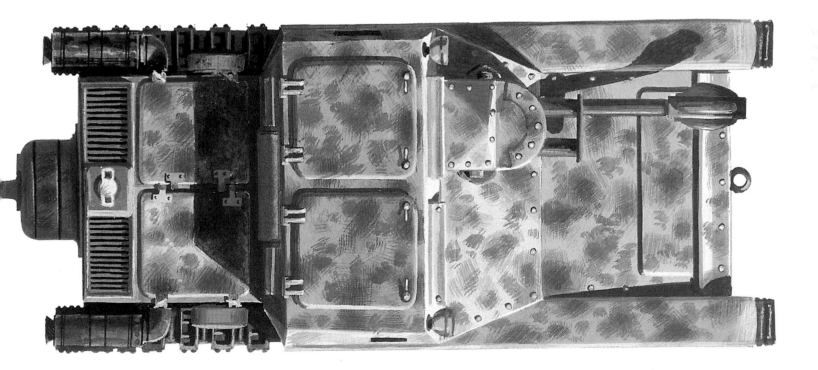

Semovente DA 75/18 Assault Gun

The Italian army relied heavily on German armoured support and built mainly light tanks during the war. By early 1943, the worsening war situation as far as Italy was concerned led to the cessation of most tank production in favour of self-propelled guns that could be pressed into service as tank destroyers. The principal example of this was the Semovente M42 series mounting a variety of guns, mainly of 75mm (2.9in) calibre. The basis for these vehicles was the Carro Armato M15/42 tank built by Fiat-Ansaldo from 1942. Only 82 of these were completed as tanks and delivered to the Italian army before the Armistice in September 1943. Two hundred Semovente with the short 75/18 (75mm/2.9in, 18 calibres) gun were ordered in March 1943 and an order for another 500 with a 75/34 gun soon followed. Trouble with the mounting of the 75/34 prevented its earlier introduction. The Semoventes dispensed with the high turret and the superstructure of the M15/42 and replaced them with a box-like fixed riveted structure with no commander's cupola. Turret access was through a large hinged hatch cover which opened to the rear. A machine-gun was stowed inside and could be mounted on the forward lip of the hatch for anti-aircraft defence, leaving the gunner rather exposed. The engine was a V-8 petrol unit of 143kW (192hp). Early versions of the M15/42 tank had a lower powered, but also lower-maintenance diesel unit, but diesel supplies to the Italian front became increasingly

unreliable and petrol engines were substituted. In September 1943 the Germans confiscated all the Italian armour that was in their area of control and took over the factory. In German service, the Semovente was renamed Sturmgeschütz M42 mit 75/18 850(i), or StuG M42. Including vehicles built by the Germans, 294 were issued to Wehrmacht infantry, Panzer, Panzergrenadier and Panzerjäger divisions in Italy and the Balkans in 1943 and 1944. By the end of the latter year, 200 of these had been destroyed, captured or were otherwise out of service. The improved M43 105/25 was completed in smaller numbers, but sported a much more effective 105mm (4.1in) gun. It likewise saw most service with the German army.

Specification

Country of Origin: Italy
Main Armament: One 75mm (2.9in) StuK 75 L/18 cannon
Secondary Armament: One 8mm (0.3in) MG 38 machine-gun
Combat weight: 15 tons
Length: 5.04m (16ft 6in)
Width: 2.23m (7ft 4in)
Height: 1.85m (6ft 1in)
Road Speed: 38km/h (24mph)
Road Range: 230km (143mls)
Crew: Three

Type 95 Kyugo Light Tank

The Japanese made no tanks effective in tank-versus-tank combat and failed to employ the tanks they did have in more than penny-packet quantities. One of the most common Japanese tanks was the Type 95, known to the manufacturer as the Ha-Go and the Army as the Kyugo. Accepted in 1935 (hence the Type 95 designator in reference to the 95th year of the current Imperial era) this tank was one of the oldest designs to see service throughout the war. Based on the Type 94 tankette, itself a virtual copy of a British Carden-Lloyd design, the Type 95 was inadequately armed and armoured and suffered from several unacceptable design flaws. The Type 94 with armour from 4–12mm (0.1–0.4in) was said to be vulnerable even to rifle fire; on the Type 95 this was increased to a minimum 6mm (0.2in) thickness, but it still could be defeated by light weapons. One was reported disabled by a 0.303 bullet strike on the idler wheel mounting. M4 Shermans frequently blew holes right through them with their 75mm (2.9in) guns. The Type 95 had intakes vulnerable to petrol bombs, and the turret could be jammed with an infantryman's knife blade. The one-man turret, in which the gunner had no seat, had a total traverse of only 45 degrees. In theory the rear facing machine-gun covered the aft hemisphere, but even then there were large gaps in the field of fire. Vision was extremely poor despite numerous open vision slits, which were not of the glass block type, increasing crew vulnerability. The three-man crew included a bow machine-gunner who also acted as general mechanic. Japanese tanks were good for causing terror among the populace in places like Manchuria and for patrolling jungle roads in Burma and the Philippines, but were never concentrated enough to have any effect against Allied armour in any Pacific invasion. Only one tank per four-tank platoon was equipped with a radio and if that was knocked out, the platoon tended to collapse into confusion. When the Soviet Union declared war on Japan in August 1945, their T-34s tore through what little opposition the Japanese tank divisions could mount with their 37–57mm (1.5–2.2in) guns and light armour.

Specification

Country of Origin:	Japan
Main Armament:	One Type 94 37mm (1.5in) cannon
Secondary Armament:	Two Type 91 6.5mm (0.25in) machine-guns (one bow-mounted, one rear-facing in turret)
Combat Weight:	7.6 tons
Length:	4.38m (14ft 4in)
Width:	2.05m (6ft 9in)
Height:	2.18m (7ft 2in)
Road Speed:	46km/h (28mph)
Road Range:	160km (100mls)
Crew:	Three

In the latter part of World War I, the French developed some of the first truly practical tanks as we know them today. For the most part, however, they failed to capitalise on their lead in tank design, believing that the next European war would be fought along the same lines as the last. The Char (tank) B1 bis (improved) was a case in point, designed with a long track that circled the hull sides for the greatest ground contact and thus trench crossing ability. The specification for a heavy tank was originally issued as early as 1921, but it was five years before this was agreed in final form and another nine before Renault's winning design was put into production as the Char B1. Despite its protracted development and outdated concept, the Char B1 had heavier armour (up to 60mm/2.3in thick) and heavier armament than the majority of tanks outside the Soviet Union at the beginning of the war. The hull-mounted 75mm (2.9in) was intended as a close-support weapon (the turret was for dealing with enemy tanks). The driver aimed the main gun by positioning the tank, with the help of an ingenious hydrostatic gearbox, elevated it if necessary and fired it. In a head-on battlefield encounter this might have worked, but most often the nippier German tanks or the long-range 88mm (3.5in) anti-tank guns scored hits on the thin side armour before the Char B1 could align itself. The commander in the one-man turret was overloaded, directing the driver and loading and firing the 47mm (1.8in) gun. Maximum range could only be achieved in low gear at a painful 10–11km/h (6–7mph). The bis was the second production variant 1 an was identified by a longer turret gun. Each of the four French armoured divisions created by May 1940 had two battalions each of about 35 of these heavy tanks. Before long these were in disarray and the surviving Char B1s were carted off to become driver training tanks for the German army. A few were pressed into service as the Panzer B-2 740(f) and served on Jersey and elsewhere.

Specification

Country of Origin:	France
Main Armament:	One 75mm (2.9in) howitzer
Secondary armament:	One 47mm (1.8in) cannon, one 7.5mm (0.3in) machine-gun
Combat weight:	32 tons
Length:	6.37m (20ft 11in)
Width:	2.50m (8ft 2in)
Height:	2.79m (9ft 2in)
Road Speed:	28km/h (17.4mph)
Road Range:	180km (112mls)
Crew:	Four